REDEEMED

ALSO BY HEATHER KING

Parched

REDEEMED

A Spiritual Misfit Stumbles Toward God,
Marginal Sanity, and the Peace That
Passes All Understanding

HEATHER KING

VIKING

VIKING
Published by the Penguin Group
Penguin Group (USA) Inc., 375 Hudson Street, New York, New York 10014, U.S.A. • Penguin
Group (Canada), 90 Eglinton Avenue East, Suite 700, Toronto, Ontario, Canada M4P 2Y3 (a
division of Pearson Penguin Canada Inc.) • Penguin Books Ltd, 80 Strand, London WC2R
oRL, England • Penguin Ireland, 25 St. Stephen's Green, Dublin 2, Ireland (a division of
Penguin Books Ltd) • Penguin Books Australia Ltd, 250 Camberwell Road, Camberwell,
Victoria 3124, Australia (a division of Pearson Australia Group Pty Ltd) • Penguin Books India
Pvt Ltd, 11 Community Centre, Panchsheel Park, New Delhi – 110 017, India • Penguin Group
(NZ), 67 Apollo Drive, Rosedale, North Shore 0632, New Zealand (a division of Pearson New
Zealand Ltd) • Penguin Books (South Africa) (Pty) Ltd, 24 Sturdee Avenue, Rosebank,
Johannesburg 2196, South Africa

Penguin Books Ltd, Registered Offices: 80 Strand, London WC2R oRL, England

First published in 2008 by Viking Penguin, a member of Penguin Group (USA) Inc.

10 9 8 7 6 5 4 3 2 1

Copyright © Heather King, 2008
All rights reserved

Portions of this book first appeared in *The Chattahoochee Review, Commonweal, Notre Dame
Magazine,* and *The Sun.*

Grateful acknowledgment is made for permission to reprint an excerpt from "The
Annunciation" by Rainer Maria Rilke from *The Unknown Rilke: Expanded Edition,* translated
by Franz Wright. Copyright © 1990 by Oberlin College. Reprinted by permission of Oberlin
College Press.

LIBRARY OF CONGRESS CATALOGING IN PUBLICATION DATA

King, Heather, 1952–
    Redeemed : a spiritual misfit stumbles toward God, marginal sanity, and the peace that
passes all understanding / Heather King.
        p. cm.
    ISBN 978-0-670-01863-5
    1. King, Heather, 1952– 2. Catholics—Biography. 3. Christian biography. I. Title.
    BX4705.K496A3 2007b
    282.092–dc22
    [B]   2007035508

Printed in the United States of America
Designed by Carla Bolte • Set in Celeste

For my nephew Allen

ACKNOWLEDGMENTS

If you really want to see the light of Christ, you have only to look at my friends: loyal and true; creative, funny; and above all, kind. So thanks to the following: Joan Biggs, Maudie Simmons, Hilary Beane, Sissy Boyd, Julia Gibson, Ellen Slezak, Marjorie Sa'adah, Patrick Kerr, Brad Valdez, Terry Richey, Clam Lynch, Glenn Lindsey, Martha Gehman, Fred Davis, Joe Keyes, Josh Kun, Barbara Fleck, Ron Stringer, and Rachelle Zazzu. Long-distance buddies Ellen Mugar, Ben Foster, Timmy J. Smith, Marisa Quien, and Mary Benson. To the ever-faithful, gloriously agitated, uber-hospitable folks at the L.A. Catholic Worker; Father Jarlath and the parish of St. Thomas the Apostle; Sara Sarasohn, crackerjack producer/editor at NPR's *All Things Considered*: we did some beautiful commentaries together. To Paul Dietrich, a bolt-from-the-blue mentor, stimulus, and help in every way; my wondrous and forbearing family; the Cushings, always; and Timothy Arthur Brown, the best ex-husband a gal could have. To Ann-Kristin Rosenberg: there'll be stars in her crown. To my agent, Laurie Liss, and my wonderful editor Carolyn Carlson; the Dorland Mountain Arts Colony, the Helene Wurlitzer Foundation, and the Ucross Foundation. To my beloved Ann Leary, a perpetual surprise, comfort, and delight. And last and most, to the folks in the back room at the Tropical Café, who save my life and give me a life day after blessed day.

Blessed be the Lord who has shown me
the wonders of his love
in a fortified city.

—Psalm 31:21

REDEEMED

INTRODUCTION

The Christian religion is only for one who needs infinite help. That is, only for one who feels infinite anguish. The whole earth can suffer no greater torment than a *single* soul. The Christian faith—as I see it—is one's refuge in this *ultimate* torment. Anyone to whom it is given in this anguish to open his heart, instead of contracting it, accepts the means of salvation in his heart.

—Ludwig Wittgenstein

I don't know about you, but this is the kind of quote that makes me feel right at home. This gives me hope. Anguish, torment—this Wittgenstein is a man who understands. So do Maria Callas, Renaissance painter Matthias Grünewald, and the people in charge of adorning Mexican churches. I love a good statue of Jesus with a hole ripped in his chest and his sacred heart hemorrhaging blood. Nobody knew better than Christ that people to whom everyday things like holding a job or interacting with another human being are never-ending sources of torture and anxiety are exactly the ones most in need of healing. A guy who hung out with lepers, paralytics, the possessed: this is someone I can trust. We don't have to go up to him, he comes down to us. We want a doctor, a hospital, meds; he gives us himself. We want to stop the suffering; he says, *I'll suffer with you.*

Like many children of the '60s, I grew up not believing in much of anything. This was through no fault of my decent, hardworking, self-sacrificing (if ever so slightly overburdened) parents. My father was a bricklayer who worked his fingers to the bone to support my seven brothers and sisters and me. My mother was a housewife who sent us all to Sunday school at the Congregational Church across the street, played hymns on the piano, and (no doubt desperately trying to stave off the inchoate sense that half of us would grow up to be alcoholics and/or addicts) was given to sayings like "Pride goeth before a fall" and "The road to hell is paved with good intentions." In white Anglo-Saxon, pre–Vatican II, Protestant New Hampshire (I was going to add "rural," but that would have been redundant), Catholicism was for Italians. Catholicism was for people from May-ass ("Mass," short for Massachusetts) who smoked cigarettes and had plastic Marys on their dashboards. Catholicism was for rollicking Irish families, not shut-down, inward-looking, abstemious, frugal, non-risk-taking folks such as us.

As a kid, and for a long time afterward, my basic idea toward God was: if I follow the rules—if I'm good—he won't hurt me. Now I see that's the whole problem. In fact, trying to be good in a way makes me bad, makes me dishonest. Whereas if I just face that I'm a sinner from the ground up—I'd sell my mother's soul for a drink, some sugar, fifteen minutes of sex—I might actually start to get somewhere. Alcoholics and addicts know this kind of thing about themselves, which is why, in spite of their other myriad shortcomings, they tend to be the funnest, and often oddly spiritual, people on earth. Of course I would think that, being one myself. In fact, I have a theory that all addiction is, at bottom, a search for God. Think about it: the blackout—a crude form of mystical union; the willingness to sacrifice reputation, family, money, health, one's very life—a twisted martyrdom. Sometimes I think anyone as drawn as I am to suffering would have *had* to become a Catholic. But truly, it's a gift to have seen the depths to which I'll fall, the extent to which I'll compromise myself, the lengths to which I'm willing to go to avoid God. The problem with avoiding God is that next thing I know, I've latched onto something outside myself, established a substitute God; and he, she, or it is holding me in complete bondage. To me, the Fall doesn't mean I'm bad (though in one way I actually am pretty bad) and that God hates me. It means I'm broken and I need help.

Alcoholism is an interesting phenomenon. It's the universal perverse tendency toward self-sabotage, except taken to the nth degree. Normal people look at an alcoholic and think, *She drinks like me—just more.* But it's a difference in kind, not degree: for the person predisposed to alcoholism, the very first drink begins setting up a mental obsession and physical craving—in essence, a form of insanity—that is entirely beyond the normal drinker's ken. Alcoholic drinking is only a symptom—of a soul divided deeply against itself; of mental, emotional, and, above all, spiritual conflict. The conflict is of a soul in which the universal human thirst for connection, meaning, love has gone terribly awry—a soul in the grip of a compulsion that has seized upon a substitute for love and made it into a god. Everybody's spiritually sick to one degree or another, of course, but what's interesting about alcoholism is that if I don't tend to my spiritual sickness, I'll die. I'll pick up a drink, or a crack pipe, or a Xanax or three million, and die. Or I'll kill myself. Or I'll get so crazy someone else will kill me. It's a condition that, over the years, has tended to grab my attention. As one of my sober friends says, "I'm not on a spiritual path because I'm so spiritual. I'm on a spiritual path because I'm so *not* spiritual."

And while following the rules isn't in and of itself the answer, once on the spiritual path, I *do* follow certain principles, certain rules. I follow the rules not out of fear but out of gratitude: for having gotten sober, for the ability to walk, see, breathe; for life. The irony is that I find when I'm on fire with gratitude, I'll not only refrain from cheating, lying, and stealing: I'll do way more than that. "Do not think I have come to abolish the law or the prophets; I have come not to abolish but to fulfill," Christ said (Matthew 5:17), and I think what he meant was that I'll live in a whole different way. I'll "waste" time, commit crazy acts of generosity, interact with all manner of extremely unpromising people. I'll quit the job I hate and, though scared senseless, start doing the work I've wanted to do my whole life. I'll put up with years and years of failure, rejection, poverty, because I'm doing something I believe in, that I love. I'll get out of the relationship that's killing me, over and over again, and finally, finally, *finally* discover it wasn't the relationship, it was me, and it's not his fault, and my mother did the best she could, and it's nobody's job to make me happy, I have to do it myself, and lo and behold, it turns out, I *want* to do it myself; that's *all* I want. I'll be like Zacchaeus, the puny publican who climbed the sycamore to get a glimpse of Jesus (Luke 19:1–10): willing to make a fool out of myself, to be enthusiastic.

But when I'm enthusiastic, when I extend a hand to the next person, I can't do it from the level of "I'm up here and you're down there." I do it because I realize I need it just as much as he or she does. I "boast of my weakness," as St. Paul did (2 Corinthians 12:9), because I can hardly believe—clueless and fallen as I basically still am—that I'm in even marginally good enough shape to help someone else, to be kind to someone else. That's the only point of the spiritual path: to get in good enough shape so I can help someone else. But not like the Pharisee who stood at the front of the church, regarded the lowlifes in the back, and said, "Thank you, God, for making me so perfect, and man, am I glad I'm not as screwed up as *they* are" (Luke 18:9–14). I have to be like the tax collector who stood at the back of the church, hanging his head, and said, "Oh my God, I can't believe you even let me in, I can't believe there's a place for me. Thank you so much and please forgive me and help me to be better."

But why do you need God for any of that? you might ask. Why not just be better—love your neighbor as yourself—on your own? Because personally, I'm too scared, too lazy, too selfish to be better on my own. I *want* to be better but the fact is I get real bored, real fast, unless I am getting a ton of approval and attention. I like to dress it all up and hedge it all around and try to hide it, but my *basic* stance toward all human beings is: what can you give me? I have a kind of spiritual adviser who helps me look at my . . . I'd like to say "issues," but they're really more like massive, glaring defects. If I'm stuck, this woman will often have me write about it as a way to help me see where I might have been wrong, where I haven't let go, where I need to pray. Recently I wrote what I secretly thought was a masterly analysis of the troubling situation at hand. It had pathos and humor, it had corollaries and tributaries, it had a quote from Dostoyevsky. I was halfway through reading this gem of a screed to her over the phone when she interrupted me. "But were you selfish?" she asked. Man, was I pissed. *Selfish? She totally* did not get it! I should *never* have tried to explain myself to someone who was not *nearly* as smart as I. She did not even begin to grasp how complicated the thing was, how multilayered, how deep. It took me two days of inner raving, ranting, seething before I realized: I'd been selfish.

But if you need God, then why Christ? you might ask next. Why not an abstract God, a God who's somewhere out in the ether, a God who's more or less an idea, an abstraction? Maybe because the word "religion" comes from the Latin *religare,* which means to reconnect; and to reconnect I first have to feel the full pain of my own separation: this aging body I'm afraid and ashamed of; my brain, which can't seem to stop running in compulsive ruts; my heart, which keeps lurching open and snapping shut at exactly the *wrong* times. I don't know myself and I'm afraid of myself and I have to come to terms with that before I can even begin to love anyone else. To me, the most incredible and best possible news about the Incarnation is that it means God isn't out there, he's in here. He's with me as I drive around the streets of L.A. thinking, *Am I the only one who thinks they're doing it this wrong, whose love life has been such an abysmal failure, who is capable of acting like such a lame, pathetic baby?* He's with me as I sit in front of my computer thinking, *Am I the only one who's trying so hard and getting such meager, paltry*

results? He's with me on my bed at night as I wonder, *Will anyone be with me when I die?*

But mostly he's with me as I wander around the streets of
L.A., mulling over snatches of Gospel, snippets of Psalms, tail
ends of parables: all the detritus of my Christ-steeped subconscious that (I can never tell when or where) will lead to some
unexpected reflection—like the distinction between pleasure
and joy. One day not long ago, for instance, my friend Joan
called, crying. Joan had just come out of and was trying to work
through the aftermath of a teensy decade-long love affair/obses-
sion with a married man. Over the years, we'd hashed it over
ad infinitum, examined it from every angle—the midafternoon
trysts, the lonely holidays, the endless disappointment and
hurt—but this time our conversation took a different turn. This
time, between sobs, she said, "Heather. A really weird thing just
happened. For the first time since I've known him, I—I thought
of his wife. For the first time ever, I felt *bad for his wife.*"

Pleasure is shallow, but joy has pain in the middle of it. Pleasure comes and goes, but joy has eternity in it. Pleasure would
have been if the married man left his wife and bought Joan a
giant diamond. Joy was this dear, dear friend of mine—who is
recovering from alcoholism and bulimia; who has struggled with
learning disorders, workaholism, compulsive money hoarding;
whose mantra is "My life is unmanageable!"; who in spite of two
marriages according to her has never had a "real" relationship—
forgetting herself long enough to feel a moment of compassion
for the (thankfully unsuspecting) wife. That, to me, is Christ:
when everything in you longs to be comforted, soothed, held, to
do those things for someone else. When everything in you longs

to be understood, to try to understand someone else. You don't have to call it Christ, and I'm sure he doesn't care if you call it Christ, but it's that stab of joy that hints at a world hidden within this one, beyond this one, where the very real suffering of this world acquires dignity and meaning and goes out, transformed, to lay the foundations of a new one.

Joan didn't stop there: as a way of making things right, she found a women's homeless shelter, operated by Vietnamese nuns, and began volunteering there once a week. It's not like she wasn't still dying for a boyfriend, but between therapy, the dentist, the meeting for people with food issues, and the nail salon, she schlepped there every Tuesday—her day off—anyway. And she ended up getting such a kick out of her time at the convent, and the Vietnamese nuns got such a kick out of her time at the convent, that three years later, she's still there. Every time she mentions it, I think, *That is loving yourself and loving your neighbor in action.* That is the paradox Mother Teresa described as "the joyful participation in the sorrows of the world."

It hurts to participate, to keep our hearts open when we're in anguish, but, as Wittgenstein observed, *this is the means of our salvation.* This is Christ nailed, arms open, to the cross, simultaneously utterly vulnerable and utterly powerful: the most radical, subversive, never-endingly surprising Savior I can imagine. Turning, in his own agony, to the thief beside him to say, "This day you shall be with me in Paradise," he's the Great Physician, the Great Priest, the Great Friend. When I picture Christ, though, he's not only, or even mostly, on the cross. He's coming down off the cross, walking among us. He's saying, *I know, it hurts unbelievably most of the time, but look, here's how to make it better.* He's saying, *Don't worry, you won't see how for a while, but it's all gonna come together in the end.* He's saying, *It's all right already: right here, right now.* He's here to help, he's here to help. Not a pious image, but a pulsing heart. A warm body. Blood.

CHAPTER 1

He has gone out of his mind.

—The neighbors, about Christ (Mark 3:21).

In 1990—sober at last—I got married, moved from Boston to Los Angeles, took the California bar exam, and started working as a lawyer. Since I'd been sitting on a barstool for the better part of the previous decade, this last, in particular, was a major, major shock. It wasn't just that at the age of thirty-eight, with the exception of two years as a real estate title examiner, I'd been a waitress all my life. It wasn't just that my office was in Beverly Hills: quite a change from the North End dives where I'd been hanging out for years. It wasn't just the hideously intimidating business of defending depositions in high-rise, fortresslike conference rooms, or asking extensions from judges I just *knew* could see through to my former degenerate life, or arguing motions at the downtown Superior Courthouse against the city's, if not the nation's, top-notch lawyers. It was that these were the people *in charge*. These were the arbiters of Truth, Justice, Right. These were the people who the rest of the world looked up to, who had been educated at the finest universities, who represented the supposed cream of democracy—and they were some of the most miserable, venal, and mean people I'd ever met. They lied, withheld, equivocated. They oozed boredom, irritation, contempt. Now I know there are good attorneys—because there are good people everywhere—and I ran into some of them in the course of what turned out to be my mercifully short-lived legal career, but for the most part the ones I saw seemed to have been leached of all morality, vitality, and fun. I thought *I'd* been cynical in my former life, squandering my talents, sleeping around, smoking cigarettes, and swilling Sea Breezes at 8 A.M. in Sullivan's Tap, but being a lawyer in L.A.: this shook me to my core.

I'd gotten my law degree essentially in a blackout, but even in my alcoholic fog, I'd felt a grudging respect for my area of study. *The law, The Law!* I kept thinking, as if the people who practiced it were privy to the secrets of the universe. I spent my first three months in L.A. studying for the California bar exam and the two months after I passed it looking for work. I had always secretly suspected that everyone but me had been handed a rule book at birth; now, finally, I would be at the very heart of how and why things worked. Now that I'd joined up and become a citizen, I could finally start to get a handle on those ideals I was starting to wonder about: Truth. Justice. Right.

That, however, was before I landed a job at the law offices of Frank L. Nee. Frank, a sole practitioner, was a cigar-smoking bachelor eight years my junior who specialized in personal injury and employment discrimination. This being Beverly Hills, I'd pictured state-of-the-art decor, communications, and supplies. Instead, the "firm" featured mauve wall-to-wall carpeting, Monet lily-pad prints, and a coffee table strewn with year-old copies of *Fortune* and *Sports Illustrated.* The computers were outdated and the dingy kitchen contained a Mr. Coffee and ancient mircrowave. I did, at least, have my own office. The floor was heaped with rolled-up exhibits, the wafer-board walls were marred with nail holes, and the windows faced south, affording, on rare smog-free days, a glimpse of the ocean and, during the 1992 riots, a panoramic view of the city going up in smoke.

I'd known the leap into lawyerdom would change my life, and I was right: the place was in a state of such stupendous disarray I didn't take a lunch break for six months. I wrote appeals from cases that had been dismissed because the statute of limitations had run, motions for relief from defaults that had been entered because nobody had sorted the mail, oppositions to summary judgment motions that were unwinnable because the boss had never gotten around to conducting the appropriate discovery. Having been lulled by law school into thinking that lawyers pondered interesting questions about chains of causation and the formation of contracts, I kept thinking, *When am I going to get to do some* real *legal work?* After a while, however, I realized this was what real lawyers did their whole lives.

Still, I yearned to contribute and, once I started to get the hang of it, saw that we could reduce workplace stress, increase the chance of winning cases, and promote cooperation with clients, court clerks, and other attorneys by the simple expedient of adopting a rudimentary form of organization. Although hardly an original idea, it seemed never to have occurred to Frank that timeliness and careful calendaring alone would have eliminated 90 percent of the crises under which we constantly labored. Envisioning proudly the way my contribution would make things easier for everyone, I devoted all my energy to not missing deadlines, not asking for extensions, not making the secretary stay late.

Unfortunately, nothing could have impressed Frank less, and I never quite recovered from the shock that he found my best, most sacrificial efforts barely worthy of notice. Instead, he viewed me as a pitiful crackpot, and I got stuck doing not only my own work but the work of Eric, the toadying paralegal, as well. Eric had a bald spot and clammy hands, twiddled a knockoff Mont Blanc pen, and wore blazers with gold insignia over the breast pocket, like the captain of a yacht. He considered himself an expert on the American legal system and everything connected with it. He belittled judges, second-guessed lawyers, and aired long-winded opinions on the ways in which the law should be rewritten and administered. He rated the intelligence of various justices of the United States Supreme Court, held forth on the science of jury selection, and critiqued the performance of the city's top trial lawyers.

In lieu of working, Eric wrote memos to Frank, filled with suggestions of work *I* could do, that began, "Your Royal Highness," and ended, "I await your bidding." Eric—who used the pronoun "we" when I had done the work, and "I" when he had contributed any part, however small—couldn't be bothered with details like deadlines and procedural rules, filling out forms and information gathering, which constitute the lion's share of labor in a law office. That, with the approval of His Royal Highness, fell almost exclusively to me. One Sunday afternoon as I singlehandedly assembled eighteen sets of exhibits, Eric lounged in my office doorway and sighed, "I *told* him to get me a lawyer!"

The person didn't exist who could have annoyed me more,

craving as I did a hundred percent of all available adulation, acknowledgment, and appreciation for myself. To make matters worse, I could scarcely have been more temperamentally ill suited to the confrontational world of trial law. Even *agreeing* with people makes me nervous, which made every conference call, verbal negotiation, and, especially, court appearance the psychic equivalent of scaling a Himalayan crevasse. Although I neurotically overprepared for even the simplest status conference, in my mind it was always a crapshoot as to whether I'd make it to the counsel table or collapse en route and have to be led away to the county psych ward. All my life I've been a bookish, easily overstimulated loner: it takes me a while to work up to any kind of human-contact activity, then the activity takes place, then I have to go off by myself for a while and process it. Those hours in court, waiting for my case to be called, were the times when I felt most keenly the absurdity of my position; when my mind on its panicked course considered the insanely wide gulf between what I would have liked to have been doing—which was sitting in a corner by myself reading poetry—and what I was actually doing; when I was overcome by a sense of alienation so acute I had to restrain myself from turning to touch the face of the person beside me.

I could have borne all this better if I'd felt I was getting a grip on that essential truth I longed for, but the actual practice of law, as opposed to the abstractions of law school, only plunged me deeper into confusion. The adversarial system of civil law is based on the curious notion that the surest way to *reveal* the truth is to place people in an artificial stance of polar opposition and give them advocates who are ethically obliged, by the concept of client confidentiality, to *conceal* the truth. "Discovery" is the process whereby each side is permitted to request, and the other is bound to produce, all relevant information, and while this was supposed to level the playing field and yield up a measure of justice, the idea that lawyers were actually going to sift through the evidence and, guided by the honor system, deliver into the hands of an opponent the rope with which to hang their own client was ludicrous beyond all imagining.

We were also pledged by the Rules of Professional Conduct to "zealously advocate" on behalf of our client. Zealous advocacy, I soon learned, meant that when a black man got fired for physically attacking a coworker, we denied the attack, claimed the client had placed his hand against the coworker's shoulder to steady himself after inadvertently slipping, and sued everyone in sight for racial discrimination. It meant that if our client had been caught throwing bulk mail into a Dumpster, we claimed it was because she'd been sexually harassed, filed a Title VII claim, and won $400,000.

Any allusion to right and wrong, any attempt to acknowledge the existence of gray areas instead of blindly insisting on black-and-white, any suggestion that the other side had a certain point, or that our own client was not entirely innocent—any reference, in other words, to the truth—was the ultimate taboo. In fact, the entire legal profession was so driven by the fear of not winning enough money, so intent on covering its ass, so inured to the meaninglessness of the whole enterprise, that if the truth had stood up from the jury box and waved, we would have stared for a moment in shock, then made a motion in limine to rule it inadmissible.

The knowledge that I had ever believed The Law to be the heart of how things worked, that after all the suffering I was enduring by forcing myself to practice it, I only felt more lost and disenfranchised than ever, filled with the same kind of anguish I'd experienced in the worst days of my drinking. I've always been lonely, but I'm not sure I've ever felt as lonely as I did when I was working as a lawyer: even my clothing—boa constrictor pantyhose, cruelly pinching high heels—seemed oppressive. On my lunch hour, I escaped the office and wandered the residential streets around Burton Way, searching the faces of the people I passed for a smile, a nod, a glance of recognition. In a deserted park, I sat staring numbly at a bed of yellow lilies, as if trying to suck strength from their sunny petals and green leaves. I passed the playground of an elementary school and paused, saddened, to think of what the adult world had in store for those carefree children. "Don't go to law school," I longed to shout over their seesaws and hopscotch games. "Whatever you do, don't go to law school!"

Underlying every other loathsome aspect of my job was the fact that I hated Eric with a black and festering hatred. I burned with it, writhed with it, fanned the flames of it morning, noon, and night by pinpointing, categorizing, and analyzing his infinite character defects: his stupidity, his cunning sloth, his soft, sluglike hands. Behind my closed office door, I worked on it like a sculptor working molten wax: a mass of indignities and slights, whose contours I endlessly, obsessively reshaped.

Since getting sober, I had embarked on a vaguely defined spiritual journey. For years I had felt everything about the world was wrong. Now, I felt everything about *me* was wrong. If legal work seemed irrelevant and boring, I told myself, it was a defect in me: it was *my* fear, *my* reluctance to enter "the straight world," *my* arrogance that had always made me different and alone. Since the age of six, when I'd first learned to read, one desire had dogged me: I wanted to write. It was the one idea that had hovered always on the edge of consciousness, that my drinking and drugging had never entirely squelched. It wasn't squelched now, but it was a pipe dream, I realized—yet another, the biggest, in fact, of my childish fantasies.

I had a tremendous sense of having been delivered from the brink—a tremendous amount of wonder that, after 20 years of hard drinking, I was sober, married, gainfully employed. Yet as I went about this job for which a lot of people would have given their eye teeth, and at which I was making decent money for the first time in my life, the feeling persisted that something was desperately wrong; that something fundamental to reason, to my very purpose on earth, didn't add up. I'd been relieved of one kind of bondage only to deliver myself up to another, and it gnawed at my conscience; it began to torment me, day and night.

And this is the thing: when I started looking around for answers, I couldn't see any. Almost nothing in our culture validates such questions, provides any meat, gives the person worried about the state of his or her soul anything to latch onto. Some adopt left-wing politics, believing that, left to their own devices, people will be good: given my own track record, I didn't buy this for a second. Some go for health spas and yoga classes. Some subscribe to New Age maxims—follow your bliss, take the road not taken, reach nirvana—none of which quite rang true. I wasn't looking for nirvana (for once); I was looking for something that resonated with my experience. And my experience was that life is really hard, and almost unbearably lonely, and nobody "wins" in the end, and instead we pretty much bungle our way through, thinking we're doing it wrong; and I had a very deep, sort of innate distrust of anyone who claimed to have permanently transcended that.

The other part of my experience was that, in spite of all the confusion and pain, somewhere in the middle of it was a tiny tiny spark of light. It seemed to have something to do with other people, with the fact that they suffered, too: how could my heart not turn over at the thought of all the other lonely, wounded, aching people in the world who still got up in the morning, had their little breakfasts, took up their crosses? I wasn't using the word "cross" at the time, but that was the general feeling; that, and a distant, faint desire to perhaps share or participate in the burden. This doesn't seem like much of a place to start, but it was all I had (and in a way, it still is).

That I'd reached this point at all was thanks to the aftermath of my hideous run with booze. Stripped of the illusion that, left to my own devices, I would do anything besides eventually self-destruct, I'd almost been forced upon getting sober to look for something greater than myself. I was receiving so much freely given love trying to *stay* sober that I almost couldn't help coming to believe in some kind of God. To have been given a second chance made me so happy that almost inevitably I was undergoing some kind of rudimentary spiritual transformation.

There was a time—specifically, my whole life up to now—when

I would have been mortified at such phrases as "power greater than myself" and "spiritual transformation." So it helped—again, thanks to booze—to have realized the deep limitations of my intelligence, and also not to feel the need to prove my intelligence. People who don't believe in God, I've observed, are often very invested in how smart they are. They'll say, "God is for stupid people" or "I'm too smart to believe in God!" and I always think, *Okay, whatever, I'm sure you are.* I myself am no genius, but I'd graduated from law school and passed the Massachusetts bar exam in the throes of acute alcoholism, which made me confident enough in my own intelligence that I didn't feel I had to add to it by not believing in God. And I'd also been lucky enough to come face to face with something against which my intelligence availed me absolutely nothing. In the depths of my alcoholism, I hadn't cared anymore whether people thought I was smart; I'd cared about mercy.

Mercy was exactly what I'd received, and it had effected a deep psychic change. Like most alcoholics, over the course of my run I had tried to manage, control, limit, analyze, rationalize, make vows about, and periodically quit drinking, all to no avail. The beginning of the end came one day in the woods outside a friend's house in Nashville, when I did something I had never once, in all those harrowing years, done before: I fell to my knees and prayed. Some would call it coincidence that, shortly afterward, my family staged an intervention and shipped me off to rehab—but that's never what I've called it. I didn't have the words or framework to describe how my 30 days in treatment felt at the time, but it had been an experience of repentance, of the Prodigal Daughter returning home. To find the door still open, the table laid, the obsession to drink lifted, my sins forgiven—this was a religious, not merely a spiritual, experience.

I'm not sure I can describe the difference, but religion seems to involve another Person. To be concerned about the state of my soul presupposes that someone greater than myself is similarly concerned; to want to be held to my highest self presupposes that someone else—someone who knows me to my core—is doing the holding. And to repent somehow presupposes not just one human heart, but two. Oscar Wilde, disgraced and in jail, wrote what to me is the greatest of all his works, *De Profundis*, from Psalm 130, which begins, "Out of the depths, I cry to you, O Lord." One passage runs:

> Of course the sinner must repent. But why? Simply because otherwise he would be unable to realize what he'd done. . . . Christ would have said—I feel quite certain about it—that the moment the prodigal son fell on his knees and wept, he made his having wasted his substance with harlots, his swine-herding and hungering for the husks they ate, beautiful and holy moments in his life.

That was the kind of thing I reflected upon as I went about my day, driving downtown, arguing motions, dreading every minute: the jockeying for power, the rudeness, the impeccably groomed, razor-sharp attorneys who seemed to have it all figured out and struck terror into my heart. Sitting in the back of the courtroom, waiting for my case to be called, picking at the skin around my nails until they bled; then driving back to the office, sitting in my office, staring into the computer—I actually started to think I might be going crazy. Who was I, a falling-down blackout drunk, to be questioning the Law, Justice, Reason, Right? Who was I, a waitress all my life, to be looking down my nose at seventy-two grand a year? I kept thinking I should talk to my husband about the things that were bothering me but I was afraid he wouldn't understand. And way, way in the back of my mind was that whisper, that echo, that voice that kept calling, *You've always wanted to write.*

Maybe you've been in this position yourself: where you feel like something's calling you but you're afraid to listen. Afraid of what it might mean. Afraid you're crazy.

Somewhere around this time I got a brochure in the mail and decided to go on a weekend retreat. As a lonely person, I'm drawn to places where I can be even more alone, so two days at the Mary and Joseph Retreat Center in Palos Verdes sounded like a great idea. P.V. is a wealthy community at the very tip of South Bay and that Friday night when I arrived I found that the retreat house was high up on a hill overlooking the Pacific. I had a plain room with a little crucifix on the wall, and around the corner were a dining hall and a chapel; I kept crossing paths with an old priest, who had a patrician Irish face, austere but warm, and a thatch of white hair, and who I thought maybe lived there, though I couldn't be sure. It was the first time I'd ever been on retreat, and I loved having all day Saturday to read, and think, and pray, and nap, and wander around the grounds looking at the flowers.

I was up early the next morning, *willing* the dining hall to open so I could get my hands on some coffee. Since this wouldn't happen for another two hours, I set out walking and found a trail, overgrown with wild mustard and fennel, that meandered down to the ocean. Rabbits frolicked in the chaparral as I walked the trail down and back, drinking in the distant cliffs, the water, the Southern California sun, which has so much hope in it but, just beneath, an edge of sadness, too.

It was a good place to mull things over, being so close to L.A. but so far away, and my thoughts were running along these lines: *Why can't you be more grateful? Why can't you fit in like everyone else? What's wrong that you're always longing, longing, longing for things to be the way they could be instead of accepting the way they are?* By this time, I was back at the retreat center, and as I headed toward the dining hall, prowling for coffee, I ran into the old Irish priest.

I have no capacity at all for hiding my emotions; everything instantly registers on my face. We both stopped, and though I tried to smile, I knew my eyes were pleading, *I don't know which way to turn and I'm in deep deep pain.* I expected the priest—whom I had never seen before I'd arrived and would doubtless never see again—to say, if anything, "Best get a grip," or "You'll find some Kleenex in the kitchen." Instead, this lovely man, full of natural reserve, inclined his head as if he were listening very carefully, touched me gently on the arm, looked me full in the face, and said, "You're very dear to God."

In a way, Christ is just the Person who sees you when you feel like you're most invisible. In a way, Christ is just the Person who knows what's in your heart before you do. In a way, I'd come to see later, Christ is just the Person who, when you look around and think you're crazy, says: *Don't worry, you're not.*

CHAPTER 2

Seek the answer in God's grace, not in doctrine; in the longing of the will, not in the understanding; in the sighs of prayer, not in research. . . . Look not to the light but rather to the raging fire that carries the soul to God with intense fervor and glowing love. The fire is God, and the furnace is Jerusalem, fired by Christ in the ardor of his loving passion. Only he understood this who said: My soul chose hanging and my bones death.

—St. Bonaventure, *The Journey of the Mind to God*

Once I started believing in God, I couldn't imagine a time when I hadn't believed in him. I mean, just look around: the sky, a face—come on. I'd always had a contemplative bent, always had a sense that the security and groundedness I craved were not of this world. Still, I was beginning to see that spiritual transformation wasn't how I'd hoped it would be—a gentle but steady upward climb to a plateau of serenity and detachment—but rather was fitful and disorderly, lurching and stumbling, to the point where I often doubted anything was happening at all, or even wondered whether I was going backward. I was also beginning to see that believing in something greater than myself, and understanding what it or he might be, and the nature and extent of the relationship between us, was a whole other matter. I said

I believed in God, but when push came to shove, I still acted most of the time out of fear, not faith. I still spent an inordinate amount of time regretting the past or worrying about the future instead of just being present. The phrase "God's will" still tended to conjure up things like becoming a nun, or emptying bedpans for a living, or dying in a fiery car crash.

Here is one way in which I was very lucky. Tim and I were living in a little rented stucco house in a part of Culver City (home of the old MGM studios) called Palms, and we were gardening a bit, and exploring different parts of the city—the beach, the mountains—on the weekends. As I mentioned earlier, on the advice of a sober friend I'd gotten a kind of spiritual director—someone to run things by; someone to help me look at my patterns, the things I'd done that hurt myself and others; someone to guide me through the process of making those things right. This tiny practice doesn't sound like much but it revolutionized my life, or at least began to. We live in a society that glorifies autonomy. But autonomy doesn't free us from bondage to ourselves and our desires—humility does. For someone of my entrenched self-sufficiency, just being willing to admit that my judgment might not be infallible, to care enough about doing the right thing to run it by someone else first, represented a behavioral sea change.

That was one benefit. Another was the discovery that someone who was herself less than perfect was qualified to help; that she was less than perfect, in fact, turned out to be the very reason she *could* help. A professional I might have been paying to help—who'd gone to school to help, who'd *studied* alcoholism but not experienced it herself would have been one thing.

Another broken-down person like me, who was helping because she was grateful, because her own spiritual life depended on and was enriched by helping, because she wanted to freely give what had been so freely given to her was entirely another. She was doing it for free! How many relationships had I had in this world where the person didn't want something from me—even if it was something "good," like friendship? I found I couldn't have this kind of person in my life—this person with problems of her own but who, out of detached, disinterested love, was willing to offer her time and energy—and fail to have every part of my life affected by it.

A further surprise, and half the value, lay in the fact that I wasn't judging and rejecting (or not as much as usual); wasn't saying to myself at every turn, *I'm not letting that wack job tell me what to do. She can't even keep a steady job! Her boyfriend's crazy. She talks too loudly, she has bad table manners,* whatever. In fact, the woman I chose wasn't "telling me what to do": she was just patiently listening and giving me her take on things; gently reminding me that basically God was my only hope and answer. This is of course a very Catholic notion, I would come to see later; to have a kind of confessor; and to my mind, any such person you can set hands on—priest, minister, member of the laity, or anything in between—is worth his or her weight in gold. Maybe the best thing about my spiritual director was that she left me to discover whatever God I wanted. She wasn't trying to impose her idea of God on me, or explain God to me, or tell me I should, say, go to church or not go to church.

Consequently, in the paradoxical way things work, I gradually started thinking maybe I *would* go to church. As I said, I'd been raised Protestant back in New England. I hadn't gone to church since I was a child—my mother had made all eight of us kids attend Sunday school, so for years I'd been against God in general and all churches on principle. Still, Catholicism struck me at that point as almost unthinkable, strictly taboo; so I figured Protestantism was the place to start. Since Tim was as shell-shocked as I was by having moved across the country and trying to adapt to a new job (he was working as a carpenter for my older brother, a contractor)—plus, being married to a person as moody as I am would make anyone need religion—he decided, at the beginning at least, to come along for the ride.

We started by making the rounds of the churches in our neighborhood—Lutheran, Baptist, Methodist, a different one each Sunday—but they all seemed like glorified social clubs. We volunteered at an Agape-type soup kitchen, but everyone we met seemed to be fighting with each other. We went to a Unitarian church in Santa Monica, where instead of calling Jesus by name, the minister and parishioners referred to "the J word." How cornball was that? What did these people believe in? Either they didn't know or they were afraid to say. Increasingly, it seemed to me, I had to believe in *something*: not to make myself "right," or to find "the answer" (as if there was one), but to strive toward, to obey. Wanting to be "moral" wasn't enough: I could want to be moral till the cows came home, but sooner or later I'd take the shortcut; sooner or later I'd resort to justifying myself and blaming you. What did "being moral" even mean in any given situation? I'd started to wonder. I'd begun paying back my defaulted student loan, for instance, but did I really owe them *all* that interest? Okay, so some stray pads of Post-its, boxes of paper clips, and Pilot pens occasionally found their way from the office into my briefcase and home—but didn't the boss owe *me* for all that "unpaid" (I was on salary) OT? What about the morality of working at a job I loathed?

Back at work on Mondays, I carried with me always the secret of my alcoholism and the fear that it had rendered me permanently unfit for "normal" life. *Why can't you leave well enough alone?* I continued to berate myself. *Why can't you fit in like everyone else?* I was thinking about God more and more, but I felt a void at the center of my life I was ravenous to fill.

Everything important in my life that I've come to, I've come to, in one way or another, through reading. In desperation and at random, so devoid of theological grounding I wasn't even sure of the difference between the Old and New Testaments, I started reading now. I read Dietrich Bonhoeffer's *The Cost of Discipleship* followed by a chapter of Meister Eckhart. I read Karl Rahner's *Everyday Faith* and Romano Guardini's *Lord.* I read *Surprised by Joy* by C. S. Lewis, Graham Greene's *The Heart of the Matter*, and St. Teresa's *The Way of Perfection.* I read Henri Nouwen's *With Open Hands* and Evagrius Ponticus's *The Praktikos. Chapters on Prayer.* I read Thomas Merton's *Seven Storey Mountain* and *The Confessions of Saint Augustine.* I even, bit by bit, began to read the Gospels.

What struck me about the Gospels was how directly they spoke to my situation, how precisely they explained why I—and, from what I could see, everyone else in the legal profession—was so deeply miserable. They talked about giving while the basic premise of litigation was getting and keeping. They talked about letting go while litigation was about hanging on with a death grip. They said to lay down your arms, and I was in a world where every morning we girded ourselves for battle.

The world in which I worked was predicated on technical compliance with the law and stretching it as far as we possibly could. But Christ had made clear that legal codes were only *beginnings*, not ends; that the idea was to refrain not just from lying and stealing and killing, but from the thoughts—the orientation of heart—that are at the root of those actions: "You have heard that it was said to those of ancient times, 'You shall not murder'; and 'whoever murders shall be liable to judgment.' But I say to you that if you are angry with a brother or sister, you will be liable to judgment; and if you insult a brother or sister, you will be liable to the council; and if you say, 'You fool,' you will be liable to the hell of fire" (Matthew 5:21–22).

Anger and insults, of course, were the meat of our profession; even in my theologically unschooled state, I sensed it was no accident that almost immediately following that passage was a warning about the dangers of lawsuits: "Come to terms quickly with your accuser while you are on your way to court with him, or your accuser may hand you over to the judge, and the judge to the guard, and you will be thrown into prison. Truly I tell you, you will never get out until you have paid the last penny" (Matthew 5:25–26). This, too, rang true: with the toll litigation took on plaintiffs, defendants, attorneys, and everyone else involved, it seemed to me we were all paying down to the last penny, all the time.

Shortly after Christmas one year, we took on as a client a recently bereaved widow named Mrs. Prietto. Her husband had died during outpatient retinal surgery, and she'd brought a medical malpractice action against the hospital and all seven of the doctors involved. I cringed when the boss assigned me to cover her deposition, and, knowing I'd be facing eight voracious insurance defense lawyers, I drove to downtown L.A. that morning with a heavy heart.

Mrs. Prietto met me in the lobby. She'd come to the office a couple of times so I could prepare her, and I'd immediately been struck by her quiet dignity. In the elevator, I surreptitiously studied her tailored suit and beautifully upswept hair. I couldn't imagine sitting in an eye clinic, maybe thinking about where to go for lunch, only to have some guy in a white coat come out and announce that my husband had just died.

In the penthouse suite where the deposition was to take place, a receptionist led us to a teak-paneled conference room that was bigger than my apartment. At the head of the table was a paunchy middle-aged man with a greasy red face. We took our seats, and without even bothering to introduce himself, he loudly snapped what sounded like the pack of gum he was chewing, gave the high sign to the court reporter, and started firing off a volley of questions at my client: did your husband have any hobbies? He played the guitar? What songs did he play? You don't remember? Where did he buy his strings? What was the name of the street the store was on? You don't know? Were they plastic strings or steel? YOU DON'T KNOW?

Sitting at the lovely Mrs. Prietto's side, I burned incandescent with shame: I'd grown used to seeing human beings turn their backs on all that is kind and decent, but subjecting a bereaved widow to such a travesty seemed monstrous. To make matters worse, I was so intimidated by the overbearing "host" attorney and the other silently smirking seven that I almost had a coronary every time I managed an objection.

As it turned out, Mrs. Prietto was almost a caricature of the perfect client, which only spurred the opposing attorney on to further rudeness. Her husband had been choir director at Our Lady of Good Counsel church: the lawyer rolled his eyes. She attended daily Mass: he heaved an exasperated sigh. She and her two daughters visited the cemetery with flowers every weekend: the lawyer interrupted to sneer, "Have you had any *physical* complaints since your husband died?"

"Physical complaints?" Mrs. Prietto replied, bewildered. "No, it is the little things I miss. Raking leaves together, painting the house, doing errands. He used to put the gas in my car for me. . . ."

"I'm *asking* if you have any physical complaints," the attorney snarled. "Insomnia, stomach pain, backaches? Have you seen a doctor? Have you started taking any prescription medicines since your husband died?"

"I don't think you understand," Mrs. Prietto said, gathering herself as she leaned in toward his tense, sweaty face. "When my husband died it was like I had been sitting in a brightly lit room and someone, without any warning, snapped the lights off. *And they were never going to come on again.*"

In the world of litigation almost every word is calculated, but this was so real I could almost smell it: real sorrow, real grief, real love forever lost. For a second, the room went utterly still; the noxious interrogating attorney even stopped snapping his gum. Quiet, soft-spoken Mrs. Prietto had brought nine attorneys to their knees, had rendered us, finally, mute.

In the silence, a phrase floated up from nowhere to the forefront of my mind: "But many who are first will be last, and the last will be first" (Mark 10:31). That was when I saw that Mrs. Prietto didn't need an attorney. In some strange, unlikely way, she had already won.

Meanwhile, work was still hell, and the harder I drove myself, the more unbearable it became. Each day I brought a spartan lunch from home: a tiny square of cheese, a handful of dried fruit. My office had all the cheer of a prison cell; I refrained from personalizing it on the theory that the lighter I traveled, the easier I could bolt when the time came. I bowed my head in communion when I read in an attorney survey the anonymous account of a man who wept with despair each morning when he turned off the freeway exit that led to his office. One day after arguing a motion at the Pasadena superior court, I ducked into a nearby Episcopalian church to pray, soothed by the silence, the slanting light, and the scent of wax, beseeching God for the courage to give up the money I was making, to accept my failure as a lawyer, to relinquish the fear of being labeled a quitter.

Later that week, almost by accident, I came across some lines in a letter by the woman who for years had been my heroine: the (very Catholic) short-story writer and novelist Flannery O'Connor: "We are not judged by what we are basically," she had written. "We are judged by how hard we use what we have been given. Success means nothing to the Lord, nor gracefulness." I can never describe the effect those simple words had on me. If I wouldn't be judged on what I was basically—fallen, inept, confused—then maybe I could quit trying to be grateful for a job that was killing me. Maybe I could admit I'd never much cared about mainstream success. Maybe I could quit trying to use what I hadn't been given, and start using what I had.

Just before I left my job, I apologized to Eric. It seemed to me that blame, were it to be apportioned, should be along the lines of 99 percent him and 1 percent me, but I had to admit that even if he had been the world's biggest blowhard, backstabbing jackass, I had not always been a model of sisterly love either. In the end, I walked into his office, forced myself to meet his eyes, and said, "I know I haven't always been easy to get along with. I'm sorry for the times I was rude or uncommunicative." This action just about killed me; I could scarcely believe, after the hideous wrongs he had perpetrated, that the words were issuing from my mouth. True to form, he took it entirely as his due, puffing and preening in his usual obnoxious way, and made not the merest apology himself.

But when I walked back out his door, something had changed; some granite ledge inside me had been dynamited to smithereens. Eric had become just another person: not the anti-Christ, but someone almost as pathetically insecure as I. I even felt a stab of compassion remembering how, after he'd bragged for months about his "fengshui–style" apartment, a friend had helped him move and reported that he owned nothing but cheap furniture and cut-rate rugs. But mostly, I wished him well in a general sort of way and then I didn't think about him at all. For three years, I had let him hold me in bondage and I wasn't in bondage anymore.

Several years later, I published a piece about my ill-fated legal career and received in response a letter from a doctor in Illinois. "You didn't deserve to go to law school!" he said, in so many words. "You didn't deserve an education! You are a lazy, ignorant, good-for-nothing scum!" He could have been right—I'd called myself worse every day for years. But the Lord works in mysterious ways. Perhaps only a field to which I was as egregiously unsuited as the law could have finally driven me into writing.

CHAPTER 3

The spirit is not a thing we display but an activity we exercise, in favor of which we choose and on which we gamble. It exists only for him who wants it and, in wanting it, brings it into being.

—Louis Lavelle, spiritual philosopher, professor at the Sorbonne

When I first started writing, I was aflame with the notion that finally, finally, I would create! What I didn't realize was that writing would create me. Sitting alone in a room for four or five hours every day, week in, week out—musing, imagining, putting words together—changed me. It changed the way I thought, changed the way I spent my time, changed how I *thought* of time. I had only so much energy and the day only so many hours. So I began to order my day differently; when I wasn't writing, I was praying for the time and energy to write. By this time Tim and I had moved east to a different part of the city: Koreatown. We had a 1940s apartment with hardwood floors, crown moldings, hand-painted tiles, a courtyard, a balcony, and a little room off the kitchen—okay, a pantry; I called it "the conservatory"—where I set up my books and computer.

Flannery O'Connor wrote for four hours a day, so I figured I'd do the same. Right from the beginning, writing for me was a religious experience. It demanded everything I had, all my devotion and attention—unlike the grim drudgery of waitressing or lawyering, however, leaving me enriched at the end of the day rather than drained. Also right from the beginning, I sensed I might pay a price for this, that writing might be a kind of marriage. My actual marriage was turning out to be way different than I'd imagined—something I chose not to look at for the moment, or in fact for about the next ten years.

Tim and I had come from adjacent small towns back in New Hampshire, done some drinking and partying together in our early twenties, then I'd gone off to live in Boston and we'd gotten together, much to our mutual surprise, many years later. A carpenter/cabinetmaker, he'd now decided, due to a toll of old football and motorcycle injuries, to become a nurse. Tim was funny, smart, decent, hardworking, good-looking, but in some ways our marriage was beginning to feel more like a brother-and-sister arrangement. Still, I, too, was embarking on a new career. I'd landed a freelance job doing legal research to pay the bills, I had my writing—and that was all that mattered.

Meanwhile, I was still going to different Protestant churches, and still finding them wanting. Like most Protestants, or nominal Protestants who'd grown up pre–Vatican II, I tended to associate Catholicism with sin, guilt, hell, no sex, and a lot of complicated, arcane rites. But what with my reading, and reflecting, and bumbling kind of prayer—and most of all because writing had already begun to lead me to my deepest self—perhaps it was inevitable that the idea gradually formed in my mind to attend a Mass. So one fateful, seemingly unremarkable weekday at noon, I made my way up to St. Basil's Church, right up the street from my apartment.

St. Basil's is a modern building with concrete towers, skinny 3-D-colored glass windows, and a half-square-block parking lot. I'd driven or walked past it hundreds of times, but until I consulted the yellow pages for the Mass schedule, I'd never even considered going inside. I remember a bronze statue of someone who appeared to be a robed lunatic looming in the foyer (this, I later learned, was St. Paul). I remember pushing open the doors to the sanctuary and being afraid "they" 'd know I wasn't Catholic and would kick me out. I remember instinctively understanding that here was consecrated time, consecrated space; that the people who had come to worship in the middle of the day, who were kneeling, standing, praying, were part of a parallel universe that intersected with eternity. I remember the way the light shone like honey on the teakwood pews, not knowing whether or how to genuflect, not being able to follow along in the missallette.

But mostly I remember seeing Christ on the cross above the altar. I'd been seeing images of the crucified Christ all my life, but I'd never seen one in the context of Mass—of this mystery, this ritual—and I didn't exactly have a burning bush experience, but it pretty much stopped me cold. St. Basil's has a beautiful fourteenth-century Tuscan crucifix, and as I gazed up at Christ, his head drooping toward his breast, everything in me wanted to move to him: to comfort him, to touch him, to be near. I saw that like us, he was in pain and he wasn't sure why, whether it would ever end, or what it was for. I saw he'd come to address the deepest mystery of humankind—the mystery of suffering. I saw he wasn't saying we were supposed to suffer *more* than we were; he was *acknowledging the suffering we were already in.*

The other thing I remember from that first Mass: right before Communion, everybody kneeled and said: "Lord, I am not worthy to receive you, but only say the word and I shall be healed." If there was one thing I'd always known about myself, it was that I was sick—soul-sick, weary. A church that didn't sugarcoat or pretend everything was all right! A church based on mystery, awe, wonder! A church that had behind it the weight of centuries; that had as its guardians the angels and saints; that encompassed and considered equally important everyone from the towering intellect of a St. Thomas Aquinas to the wet-brain in the street. Maybe I'm remembering it wrong, but it seems to me I never teetered on the razor's edge, thinking, *Should I or shouldn't I? Let me carefully weigh this from every conceivable angle.* It seems to me I got one glimpse of Christ and thought, *Oh my God, can I come? Am I invited? Don't leave me out, please! I've felt left out all my life. . . .*

Perhaps this is the place to say that nothing in my past had prepared me to join the Catholic Church. As a youth, I'd painted "Dreams suck" and Sartre's "Hell is other people" on my bedroom wall. For much of my adult life, I'd been a down-and-dirty barfly, hanging out at the end of my drinking with washed-up cab drivers and racetrack touts. I'd always thought of spiritual people as kind, calm, intelligent, open-minded, "for" everyone and everything—and religious people as deluded, narrow-minded, fanatical haters, and in charge of the Inquisition. I'd always been a "thinker" (which I'm not saying is necessarily a virtue, believe me), always been a loner (if those traits predispose a person to be a follower of Christ, which they just might), but nobody in my family was Catholic. I didn't know a single practicing Catholic.

All the people I knew who'd been to Catholic school loathed, despised, and blamed it for their deepest psychosexual ills. I'm capable of "believing" something just *because* it's contrary, or, in a different wrongheaded way, because it's what I want to hear.

But as the weeks wore on, and I went to Mass again and again, I wasn't just believing because I wanted to. I was believing because I felt Christ in the core of my being. I was believing because I felt a stirring, as if I were falling in love. I was believing because I could suddenly see that everything in history, nature, psychology, science resonated with this universal paradigm of death and resurrection that was taking place every second, on an infinite number of levels, from the atomic to . . . I mean the *sun* is slowly dying. But Christ didn't "just" die; he came out on the other side of his suffering transformed: he was—astoundingly, cataclysmically, turn-everything-upside-down-for-all-time resurrected. Something new had been made of him, just as the longer I stayed sober, something new was almost imperceptibly being made of me. I, too, was being "reborn," not in the hokey evangelical sense, but in ways so subtle I could sometimes hardly recognize them. I didn't understand God, of course, but I understood just enough to know I was having an experience of God.

All of this sank in slowly, slowly: on my walks around the neighborhood, holed up in "the conservatory," lying in bed at night reading. I still hadn't caught on to the order and meaning of Mass, but I was continuing to be drawn by the Gospels. Outside on the streets of Koreatown, car alarms blared and helicopters whirred, but all was quiet in our little apartment. The quince tree in the back garden tapped against the glass, Tim puttered around in the kitchen, the cat slept at my feet, and there I'd be, lying in bed reading my Bible.

I could tell right away that I was not going to be a biblical scholar. I read a ton of articles and books but I could never remember when and by whom the Gospels were written (other than not too long after Jesus died) and what all the differences and similarities were (other than that John is way different than Matthew, Mark, and Luke). I sort of loved that they were all patchwork, and that people way smarter and more patient than I had gone over them with a fine-tooth comb, and argued and continue to argue over their provenance, accuracy, and meaning. Partly this was because I can be lazy, but mostly it was because my brain doesn't work that way; scholarship just isn't the kind of thing that grabs me. I read the book of John, for instance, and then I read a dense, two-volume study of the book of John by Father Raymond Brown, who was apparently an incredibly accomplished and well-respected biblical scholar, and obviously had an IQ of about 180. I took six months to plow through both volumes, and highlighted, and wrote notes in the margins, and didn't skip a single footnote, and a month after I was done the only thing I remembered was that in John 1:14, where it says, "And the Word became flesh and lived among us," "lived" really means "pitched his tent." Which slayed me, and stuck with me, and which comforts and sustains me, and gives me fruit for reflection to this day.

What also grabbed me was Christ spending 40 days in the desert, Christ preaching the Sermon on the Mount, Christ sweating tears of blood in the Garden of Gethsemane the night before he died. This was a God who was with us in our darkest human moments, who had suffered every insult, humiliation, confusion, loneliness that we have. I'd think, he knew what it is to yearn, to feel like a loser, a failure, and a misfit. He knew what it is to be tempted by the power of alcohol, or sex, or money. He knew what it is to be in emotional pain, psychic pain, spiritual pain, physical pain; to live in constant precariousness. I'd think, he doesn't know what it's like to get old. But he knew what in a way is worse than getting old, which was to watch his thirty-three-year-old beautiful body be scourged, butchered, broken, to have his health desecrated and defiled, to be cut down in the prime of life, to never *get* to be old, to die even more unfinished than a lot of us get to be. To never know what might have been.

I began to see that this God—who had the power to do anything; who commanded the sun and stars—had instead consented to empty himself and become the hardest thing in the universe it is possible to be: a mortal human being. He'd become human in order to enter into our daily lives, to be with us every waking and sleeping moment, to fulfill the deepest desire of the human heart: to not be so eternally, everlastingly alone. In a way I was becoming a believer just because Christ *did* fulfill the deepest desire of the heart: isn't it our greatest wish that God not be some faraway abstract entity, but somehow like us? That God walks among us is so simple we refuse to believe it; it so fulfills our deepest yearning we're blind to the fact that it actually *has* been fulfilled. Think of those imaginary friends we have as children, when we're still "simple" enough to think that by believing something, we can bring it into being. But that doesn't mean Christ is a fairy tale, or wishful thinking, or an illusion. We can bring things into being only by believing them with the purest of hearts. We can bring into being only the true and the real—"I am the way, and the truth, and the life" (John 14:6)—what already exists, in a sense.

I didn't have anyone to talk to about all this—Tim had lost all interest in Christianity by this time and become a Buddhist—but I'd never needed anyone to tell me how I felt about the rising of the sun. The more I read about, went to Mass to be near, and got to know Christ, the more I wanted to know him. I couldn't get my mind around a God who ruled by such apparent powerlessness. If Christ is God made man, it came to me one day, for instance, then *God lets us kill him*. He didn't, and doesn't, so much "die for our sins" as love us so much, so fiercely guard our free will, that he allows himself to be in a relationship with us *in which he is capable of being hurt*; in which he allows himself to be totally, totally vulnerable. He could have made himself impervious to hurt, but he didn't. And when we hurt him—because it did hurt, almost beyond comprehension, to be betrayed by his friends, to have his life's work go for seemingly nothing, to be scourged, mocked, scorned, to be crowned with thorns and have spikes driven through his palms, the soft part of his feet, to basically suffocate to death, publicly, with people spitting at him and jeering, which continues to happen, throughout the world, every day, as we kill the Christ in ourselves and others, revile him, commit barbarous atrocities in his name—he doesn't hold a grudge, doesn't have a word of reproach. He says, *Oh come back, you're back? Oh that makes me so happy, come over here by me and I'll tell you what I've learned, I'll show you how to be awake, alive, reconciled. . . .*

It's easy to scoff at miracles, but another thing I liked about Christ was that he never performed magic-trick miracles; he didn't pull rabbits out of a hat, or produce gold ingots. He performed the miracle of the loaves and the fishes; he made the blind see, the lame walk, the deaf hear. He performed miracles to bring people alive; he operated on a higher level of reality in order to bring love into the world. He didn't go off and sit in a cave and grant folks an audience one by one, like some wise old shaman, either; he mingled. He ate and drank with people; he touched them, human flesh to human flesh: demoniacs, lepers. And when he did heal, he never held the people up as sideshow freaks or floor models to show how great he was. He didn't bring the president of Kenya onstage to tearfully express his gratitude, such as certain megapreachers from oh, say, Orange County, California, have been known to do. As a matter of fact, he cautioned the people he healed *not* to tell anyone. Of course they did anyway, which only got him into trouble.

The small, hidden, anonymous God I found in the Gospels appealed to me deeply. It was the God I'd found in sobriety, who worked through other people, who had a sense of humor, who held me accountable and forgave me at the same time. Who didn't force or judge, just invited me to do a little better, then put the challenges in my path to teach me how. Christ subverted all worldly systems—political, familial, financial: not for the sake of being subversive, but because acting with utter integrity is automatically subversive. He was left of the furthest left and right of the furthest right, both radically liberal and radically conservative. In one breath he could say, "Honor your father and your mother" (Mark 7:10) and in another, "Let the dead bury their own dead" (Luke 9:60). On the one hand he could say, "Keep awake therefore, for you do not know on what day your Lord is coming" (Matthew 24:42); and on the other he could say,

"Consider the lilies . . . they neither toil nor spin" (Luke 12:27). Christ's way was a different kind of middle ground than that of "balance" or "health": a consenting to hold, in one's body and soul, the almost unbearable tension of opposites; to work out each unique situation on its own terms, with no hard-and-fast guidelines or rules.

In all those years of my drinking I'd told myself I hadn't believed in God, but I really had. The God I'd believed in ruled by fear, kept an account book, operated through a system of rewards and punishments. This God I was coming to believe in was calling me to the highest possible levels of truth, courage, freedom, justice, honor, and duty but was also fully human, with all a human's capacity for tenderness, with knowledge of all the pitfalls humans are prey to, with all a human's longing for beauty and meaning. Christ wasn't a philosopher like Socrates. Nailed to the cross, he didn't coolly say, "Kill me, see if I care; I've detached from the things of this world." He was in agony, as we are; he was saying, "Father, Father, why have thou forsaken me?" as we would: as I *had*, in so many words, at the depths of my drinking, in the crisis of my hideous legal career, a thousand times, still, every day.

And yet, against all odds, here I still was. Sober—and if you don't think that's a miracle, you've never been or met a practicing alcoholic. Writing—the one thing I'd always wanted to do. In L.A., where, instead of the long, hard winters I was used to, the sun shone down like a benediction. And at the doorstep of the Catholic Church, which, of all places, and after a lifelong sense of exile, was shaping up to be the truest home I'd ever known. Christ was so unlikely a Savior, the Resurrection so unlikely a "triumph," that I almost had to believe it—because for all its unlikeliness (and it seemed to me this would be true for anyone)—*it was also the story of my own life.*

As C. S. Lewis famously said of Christianity: "It is not the sort of thing anyone would have made up. It has just that queer twist about it that real things have."

CHAPTER 4

For those who abandon themselves to it, God's love contains every good thing, and if you long for it with all your heart and soul it will be yours. All God asks for is love, and if you search for this kingdom where God alone rules, you can be quite sure you will find it. For if your heart is completely devoted to God, your heart itself is this treasure, this very kingdom which you desire so ardently.

—Jean Pierre de Caussade, *Abandonment to Divine Providence*

In view of L.A.'s mixture of the sacred and the profane, somehow it seemed fitting that when the time came, I became a Catholic at the Church of the Blessed Sacrament in Hollywood. Established in 1904, Blessed Sacrament was Hollywood's first Catholic church. The parish of such Tinseltown luminaries as Irene Dunne and Loretta Young, the building featured a portico, two balconies, a terrazzo floor, imposing stained-glass windows, and a four-manual sixty-stop organ. Here, I'm proud to say—a stone's throw from the Capitol Records building, Grauman's Chinese Theatre, and Ripley's Believe It or Not! Museum ("Where truth is stranger than fiction")—I took RCIA (Rite of Christian Initiation for Adults) classes for a year, was confirmed, and made my first Communion.

Sometimes I feel half my life in L.A. consists of driving, and worrying that I'm going to be late, and trying to find a parking spot into which to maneuver my car. So every Thursday night I'd drive from Koreatown down Sixth to Rossmore, which turns into Vine north of Melrose, then west on Sunset to Cherokee, fighting the last of the rush-hour traffic on the one hand, and on the other, looking forward to meeting with Father Jim, a Jesuit priest who lived at Blessed Sacrament and was big and jolly and smart and sprawling and wore an AIDS Walk T-shirt and scruffy beard. Father Jim, the first person to whom I'd spoken when I called, was the real reason I'd chosen Blessed Sacrament. For a while I was the only person in the class, so I was getting individual instruction. From a Jesuit father!

Father Jim spoke of the Gospels with fervor and reverence, a major plus as, really, that's what I was looking for: someone for whom Christ seemed the ground of his existence, who gave the impression of having tapped into a source of inexhaustible energy, power, excitement. He instructed me to buy the *Catechism of the Catholic Church*, a thick, somewhat alarming-looking book with sections on, among other things, the Sacraments, the Commandments, and "Life in Christ." He presented me with a loose-leaf binder of essays by other Jesuit priests on subjects ranging from the order of the Mass, to the meaning of baptism, to the Church's stance on euthanasia. One was called, "What Is the Kingdom of God?" and quoted Thomas Merton to the effect that we must be rid of the ridiculous idea that if we give ourselves to God he will visit us with some horrible pox—strike us down with leprosy, for example—to test us. As a matter of fact, we have to be rid of the idea that God visits *anything* evil on us to test or strengthen us: just because he may give us the strength to get through a painful situation and learn grace from it doesn't mean that he willed the evil thing in the first place. Another essay was on the parable of the Prodigal Son, who, Father Jim observed, was not particularly remorseful when he returned home: he was just hungry—the point being that, when we return to him, God accepts us with unbounded joy on any terms.

I started RCIA classes in September. Sometime in November, a couple of other folks came around: an earnest, young, former druggie named Carl, and a lovely twenty-eight-year-old woman from Nigeria. Sophie had never been given the opportunity to go to school back in Africa so she'd come to the United States without knowing how to read or write. Six days a week she took an hour-long bus ride to her job as housekeeper/nanny in the Valley, three nights a week she attended English classes, and on one of the other nights, she had RCIA. "I so *tired* some mornings," she told me one night as I drove her home to her apartment in Silverlake after class. "And I say, 'Lawd, *hep* me to have the strenth to get through the day.' And at night, I say, 'Thank you, Lawd, for the strenth you give to me.' The prayin, it heps. Yeah."

The little study where we met was on the east side of the church, off the parking lot and down a flagstone-lined path. I'd ring the office and Rosalita would let me in, and around the corner Father Jim would be sitting behind his desk—the air smelled of lace doilies and furniture polish—with three chairs ranged around for Sophie, Carl, and me. We studied the Lord's Prayer, we studied the apostolic tradition, we studied the Nicene Creed, which was developed by the first two ecumenical councils in the fourth century A.D. and is professed by the congregation, after the homily, during Mass: "We believe in one God, the Father, the Almighty, maker of heaven and earth, of all that is seen and unseen. We believe in one Lord, Jesus Christ, the only Son of God, eternally begotten from the Father, God from God, true God from true God, begotten, not made, one in Being with the Father. . . . "

Carl and I had both been baptized in our childhood churches (the Catholic Church recognizes Protestant baptisms), which meant we were "candidates." Sophie, due to be baptized, confirmed, *and* take her first Communion, was what's known as a catechumen. Every Sunday we showed up for Mass and were dismissed after the Creed to go sit in the garden beside the church and reflect on that day's Scripture and/or whatever else came up with our sponsors—a kind and giving married couple who had a three-year-old son and ran a dry-cleaning establishment.

I'd always tended to think of the Church as rigid, but the more I learned, the more it seemed to me that Catholicism is centered in, submits to, and bows in awe before mystery: the Virgin Birth; a God who's fully human, yet fully divine; a Trinity that's simultaneously three separate entities and one. "Sacrament" is defined by *Webster's* as "something regarded as having a sacred character or mysterious meaning." The Church recognizes seven of them: Baptism, Confirmation, Penance, Anointing of the Sick, Holy Orders, Matrimony, and the Sacrament of Sacraments: the Eucharist, the Body and Blood of Christ.

The mystery of the Eucharist alone—that Christ left his Body and Blood for us to eat and drink—I could ponder forever and not fully plumb its depths. That it's his *actual* (real) Body and Blood—not "virtually real," not a symbol. That he literally becomes part of us and we become part of him. That by leaving us "food" to eat and drink, he acknowledges and appeases our ravenous spiritual hunger. That eating human flesh is the deepest, darkest, most unmentionable of taboos: not cannibalism, though, because he *gives* it. The very worst thing a human being could do—butcher a man, torture to death a person who's completely innocent, and eat him—Christ says, I'm going to *let* you do it: I'm going to offer myself up. I'm in solidarity not only with your humanity, your brokenness, your sins; I'm in solidarity with your pathologies. And in offering up my very flesh, I am going to transform the consciousness of all humanity, for all time. I'm going to descend to the depths and ascend to the heights of the human spirit and, to all who want to avail themselves, open up the possibility of becoming truly awake and alive to reality.

While I could never plumb the depths of the Eucharist—yet a simple fisherman would understand all that needs to and probably can be understood about it: it's a gift, and it's holy. Someone sacrificed himself and left his very Body and Blood to us as a gift, an offering, the answer to our deepest prayer: *Oh please let there be something beyond me and my sadly, pathetically limited powers. Let there still be something holy in the world, let there be something we haven't wrecked with our greed, our fear, our lust. Let the terrible, terrible suffering of me and every other human being on earth have meaning.* The Mass is a celebration and reenactment of the sacrifice: the consecration of the Host, the bridging of the gap between life and death, light and dark, heaven and earth, the material and spiritual. The Eucharist is the eternal coming-into-being of the power that on the one hand has the ability to shake the foundations of the universe, and on the other, perpetually, gently assures us that we are known, seen, cherished; that God hungers for us, thirsts for us.

More and more, I hungered for him, too. Candidates and catechumens are traditionally received into the Church at Easter. I'm not sure whether it was that Sophie and Carl started later than I did, or whether Father Jim and I got our wires crossed, but in around February it occurred to me that if things kept going at the pace they were, I couldn't possibly be received by April. In retrospect I see that Easter is the center of the liturgical year, that there are deep mystical, theological, and psychological reasons for coming into the Church at that time, that by insisting on coming in at some other time, I missed out not so much on the "pageantry," although that has its place, too, but on the spiritual preparation, the going down into the dark, the psychic sense of death and resurrection undergirding the long period of Lent. Whatever the case, probably because I kept bugging Father Jim, somewhere along the line, it transpired that the Church was going to make an exception for me. Instead of waiting till the following Easter, I would be confirmed and take my first Communion in August.

RCIA contains five main stages: the Period of Inquiry, the Catechumenate (both of which I'd already completed), the Period of Purification, the Paschal Triduum (the three-day Easter celebration of Good Friday, the Easter Vigil), and the Mystagogical Catechesis. The Period of Purification generally begins on Ash Wednesday. Mine started in mid-July, which, since I was on my own now, meant that for five weeks running, I was called up to the altar after the homily to stand before the congregation. At the Rite of Introduction, my female sponsor signed me with the cross—forehead, lips, ears, heart, and hands—and I proclaimed that I was there to learn, through the mystery of the cross, how and what it means to love our neighbor as ourselves. At the Rite of Election, the parish prayed over me. Then Father embraced me in his scratchy green robe and formally announced that I would soon participate in the Sacraments of Initiation. In a real Easter confirmation for catechumens, "the Scrutinies"—meant to inspire a desire for purification and redemption—are the woman at the well (John 4:7–42), the man born blind (John 9:1–41), and the raising of Lazarus from the dead (John 11:1–44). Since this wasn't Easter, my sponsors instead accompanied me to the altar two Sundays later and we all knelt during the intercessionary prayers, which that day were all directed at me.

On August 15, the Feast of the Assumption of the Blessed Virgin Mary, I made my First Confession. Father Jim showed up in his ratty T-shirt and polyester slacks, and gave a loving, generous, and clear description of the Sacrament of Reconciliation and its purpose and meaning. Then he donned his embroidered stole to make it official, and, in spite of my sin-racked life, I kept things very short. My penance was to reflect on one of the readings for that day's Mass, Ezekiel 9:1–11, which describes how God marked the good people on their foreheads, to be passed over, and commanded the others to be slain. At first glance, this did not sound very encouraging, but Father Jim pointed out this was perhaps because when we read it we tend to think of ourselves as the bad ones, while maybe the message is that the good people are "rewarded" (although when I think about how Christ's "reward" was the cross, depending on what kind of mood I'm in, that's not so encouraging either).

Finally, the big Sunday arrived. Tim and I got to the church in plenty of time and sat down in front. When it came time for me to mount the altar, Father Jim forgot the oil, necessitating a break in the service, and accidentally omitted one of the prayers. I repeated a line to the effect that I had studied and believed in all the teachings of the Catholic Church; Richard the deacon fetched the oil; Father Jim wiped some of it on my forehead; my sponsors, Richard, Father, and I exchanged the kiss of peace; and Richard said, "Welcome aboard" out of the corner of his mouth: that was the confirmation. Then I tottered back to Tim, and my pew, until I was once again called up to partake—at last!—of the Blessed Sacrament. Just this one day, they let me go first. Father Jim looked me in the eye and said, "You really are special: the Body of Christ." "A-*men*," I replied. I also had a very teeny sip of wine—"The Blood of Christ: Amen"—after which I returned calmly to my seat, and it was done.

Kneeling to pray, Christ's Body and Blood inside me, I thought of how he had come down through space, through time, through the moment I emerged from my mother's womb, through every moment I had lived, every arbitrary and seemingly wrong turn I'd ever taken, through the coast of New Hampshire, the bars of Boston, the streets of Culver City, Beverly Hills, Koreatown, to St. Basil's, to the Church of the Blessed Sacrament, with its cheesy baptismal font, its Brobdingnagian pink-veined marble columns, Father Jim, sweating in his cassock, fumbling for the oil, another human being with hands, hair, lusts, a heart.

It was the last place on earth I would have imagined ending up, and it was the only place I could have possibly ended up.

In a minute I would stand and go out to the world—to Starbucks, Staples, Frederick's of Hollywood—but for now, eyes closed, head bowed, I'd gone deep inside: the same, but transformed; the same, but irrevocably committed. "I am the good shepherd. I know my own and my own know me," Christ said (John 10:14). We had found each other, there in the pasture.

CHAPTER 5

... only her and him:
seeing and seen, eye and whatever is beautiful to
   the eye
nowhere else but right here. *This*
is startling. And it startled them both.

Then the angel sang his song.
   —from Rainer Maria Rilke's "The Annunciation"*

Back in my drinking days, I'd taken birth control pills, slept around with abandon, had abortions. It was *my* body, to do with what I wanted, and nobody else's business, I figured. So coming to terms with the Church's stance on sex represented a massive inner shift.

Actually, looking back, the shift had started even earlier. Tim and I had lived together for a year and a half, eloped to the island of Nantucket, and paid a justice of the peace thirty-five bucks to marry us—hardly the groundwork for a lifelong union envisioned by the Catholic Church. Still, almost instinctively, I'd recognized that marriage is a sacrament. I took my vows seriously, was eager

* Translated by Franz Wright, permission granted by Oberlin College Press.

to contribute, and aimed to be as faithful, helpful, and cheerful a partner as I could till "death do us part."

In a lot of ways, I loved being married: loved having someone with whom to share the daily struggles, stories, joys, and jokes of life, to eat dinner with every night, to sleep beside. And I loved being married, too, simply because it was difficult, because it did require so much compromise, because it forced me to grow. Maybe that was why, as I settled into being a Catholic, and a wife, I slowly came to see that the Church's stance toward sex did not consist of a collection of arbitrary, mortification-of-the-flesh rules, designed to diminish an otherwise "healthy," fully lived life. It stemmed from a radical overhaul of one's entire viewpoint. It stemmed from the realization that our bodies are not, in fact, our own: that no act is personal, done in isolation apart from the world. Every act has consequences; every thought, word, deed affects every other person in the universe. The point of which is not to sit around pulsating with guilt for our "bad deeds" (apparently, and deeply unfortunately, the stance of many of the schoolteacher/nuns my now-lapsed Catholic friends were taught by in the '50s and '60s), but to open up to the challenge, responsibility, and deeply startling possibility of living a life based on love.

Maybe it helped having been so promiscuous in my drinking days, and discovering that far from empowering me, sleeping around only made me feel bad about myself, men, and the world to the point of suicide. Whatever the case, I never had much trouble (which is not to say I won't in the future) with the Church's teaching of no sex outside of marriage. After years of giving myself to anybody who asked (and many who didn't), my feeling had become, *Why would I want to entrust everything that was most precious and inviolate about me to someone who wasn't fully, irrevocably committed?* The way I understood it, the Church wasn't saying sex is wrong; on the contrary, it was saying sex is sacred, it's so holy that we should be careful around it. The Church was saying that if I'm having sex with someone who's not totally crazy about me, who's not totally behind and with me, who doesn't care about me and my well-being enough to acknowledge the awesome power of sex, and the bond it forms or should form, and the emotions, hopes, expectations, tenderness, and possibility of new life it gives rise to, then we're both missing out. We're not getting anywhere near the full extent of the gift. We're missing the connection every human being longs for: to be truly known, seen, acknowledged, adored. Not that *I'd* know, having never inspired such love in anyone myself. But I've had enough of the uncaring kind of sex to know how empty it's left me, and to know it's had wide-ranging and long-lasting, if not permanent, consequences. It's left me more fearful of rejection, more distrustful, less likely to let anyone get close or to attract someone who's capable of getting close to me.

To that end, it scarcely seemed a hardship to go without mechanical/chemical forms of birth control, all of which, as it happens, impinge upon a woman's body and therefore make sex *less* free, unburdened, natural, and pleasurable (condoms should be outlawed, to my mind, simply because they're gross). As for abortion, I'd had three by the time I was confirmed, and knew instinctively when I had them, and believe even more strongly now, that abortion is wrong. It doesn't matter whether what's being destroyed is a "person" or not: it's wrong. To take the most sacred, miraculous, mysterious thing in the universe—the fruit of the union between a man and a woman, the living seed of a human being—and destroy it is wrong. I'm not saying I don't understand any number of reasons why I had, and other women have, abortions, or feel driven to abortion, or feel there's no other option but abortion, but an act of violence can never also be an act leading toward true freedom or power. We have to act as if the universe we long for is already in place, as if the kingdom of God is already here. And by believing it, and acting in accord with our belief, we bring it into being ourselves, a universe where we admit that actions have consequences and take responsibility for them; a universe where we reserve sex for people who cherish us, and vice versa; a universe where every child is welcomed. That's not to say I think abortion is murder, or should even be criminalized. In a way, it's a murder of ourselves: a murder of hope, of love, of the only reason we were put here, which is surely to care for and be kind to each other. Which is why, if I think abortion is wrong, I also have to realize that poverty, racism, and wishing the bratty kids next door would die are wrong, and start thinking about what I might do to relieve those situations.

The movement from selfish, immature love, to mature self-giving love—sexually and otherwise—is the work of a lifetime. As it turns out, the Church has a perfect model for me, particularly as a woman: the Blessed Virgin Mary. Before weekday Mass at St. Basil's began, everyone stood and a lector led what I eventually learned was a traditional prayer of the Church in honor of the Incarnation and in devotion to Mary, called the Angelus:

The angel of the Lord declared unto Mary:
And she conceived of the Holy Spirit.
Behold the handmaid of the Lord:
Be it done unto me according to Thy word. . . .

I did not have much of an idea of Mary at the time, and what idea I did have was derived from religious statuary: a plaster tinted Mary in a sterile cowl, eyes piously averted, hands clasped in prayer. I'd never heard the Angelus, and the first time I did, I thought with a start of Margaret Atwood's *The Handmaid's Tale*, a truly creepy novel about a society in which women are imprisoned and forced to bear the children of sadistic political leaders with barren wives.

The more I thought, reflected, and prayed the Rosary, though, the more I saw that Mary was an entirely different kind of handmaid. For starters, she had chosen, not been forced, to bear Christ: when the angel Gabriel appeared to this simple peasant girl, it was with a question, not a command. The operative feature of being a simple peasant girl wasn't that Mary was stupid, or gullible, or easily duped; it was that she hadn't been corrupted by the desire, as God knows I have, to be or to appear sophisticated. She was humble enough, sensitive enough, and most of all pure enough to understand that she was being invited not to have her body callously used as a vessel, but to put her entire being at the service of God. Mary was human, which meant she knew how our very identities get tied up in trying to manipulate things into going our way: we need an angel to appear and offer us entry into another world, to leave the one that consigns us to everlasting misery behind. To serve rather than be served, to conform one's will to God's instead of trying to make it the other way around: these are ideas that go so strongly against the human desire for control, safety, and security that it took a great and rare soul to understand the invitation was to freedom, not enhanced slavery. That's where Mary was when she said, "Let it be done unto me according to Thy word": not resignedly or passively, but in a way that was vital, alive, fully awake; knowing that every faculty would be tested, challenged, engaged to its utmost. In the passage known as the Magnificat (Luke 1:46–55), Mary, pregnant with Christ, makes her way to the hill country, spies her also-pregnant cousin Elizabeth, and exclaims: "My soul magnifies the Lord, and my spirit rejoices in God my Savior" . . . Humble, maybe. Grateful, courteous, generous in spirit, full of joy, yes. But oppressed, as some fellow female writers have suggested? No.

As for those who shake their heads at the simple, stupid folk who believe in the Virgin Birth, all I can say is, You've never fallen in love. Anyone who's ever fallen in love knows there's a world other than this one, a plane where staggering, inexplicable events occur. Anyone who's fallen in love knows that as stupendous, as earth-shattering, as sublime as sex is, there's something even higher. Anyone who's fallen in love knows it breaks you open, as a woman is broken open giving birth. And anyone who's fallen in love knows that it often looks like bad news, like a scandal: as Dostoyevsky said, "Love in practice is a hard and dreadful thing compared to love in dreams."

The angel and Mary in Rilke's poem both knew this; it's why they were afraid. They were afraid because they knew she was being vested with an unimaginable trust, because they couldn't know what Mary's saying yes would mean, because they knew that everything hung in the balance. The whole cosmos must have stood still, even the trees and stars holding their breath, waiting for her reply. So she'd held her own breath—and said yes. She'd closed her eyes—and said yes. She didn't have to, but she said yes. Not to man's word, but to the word of God. Not to a life free of suffering, because no such life exists, but to a life in which suffering is freely accepted as part of an ongoing creation we are not given to fully understand. Not in subservience, but in an act of faith so pure it was blinding, like an arrow shot through the eye.

Mary carried that yes in her womb, carries it still: it's the one thing under the sun that is always new, eternally new, ever fresh and surprisingly new. That yes is the "ah!" of Gerard Manley Hopkins's "Because the Holy Ghost over the bent world broods / With warm breast and with ah! bright wings." It's the "lump in the throat, a sense of wrong, a homesickness, a lovesickness," with which Robert Frost noted the writing of a poem begins. It's the self-renunciating love of the person who would rather die than yield her honor or shed the blood of another—not because self-renunciating love is soft, but because it's unimaginably steadfast and persevering and fierce. No one knew this better than Mary, for whom love in reality turned out to mean poverty, frequent anxiety, standing vigil at the foot of the cross as her son died in agony. "Stabat Mater," goes the ancient hymn: the mother is still standing. Still upright, still unwavering, still holding fast against the encroaching corruption and violence.

One of the manifestations of Christ coming into the world through a human birth is that we're connected absolutely. We're not just connected a little, or when it suits us, or is convenient.

And not just in "big" ways, either: in every way, which goes back to the real point of the Church's teachings on sex. Say you're indulging in a little Internet porn, for example: that person on the screen is a *person*. She or he has a mother, a father, sleeps at night, has hopes and dreams. So you're violating that person somehow. It doesn't matter that the person is inviting, or allowing, the violation; you're treating them, not to mention yourself, like something way less than a full person.

It's the same if you're fantasizing sexually about someone: you're getting off on thinking about someone you've met who you're maybe afraid to be with, or who doesn't want to be with you. What's the harm? you think. They're in the stream of life! you think. Is it my fault they put themselves out there and I'm attracted to them? It doesn't seem like much, but when you think about it, this is a terrible, terrible violence, a violation. The point is not so much the terribleness, but that we can't be doing that and at the same time going around complaining, Oh how heinous, how reprehensible: those chauvinist pigs and psycho-rapists and pedophile priests! As long as we're treating any other person (or ourselves) as a sexual object, we're contributing to behavior we purport to abhor; we're part of the problem. That's why Christ said if we lust even in our hearts, we're on the wrong path. The point is, again, not to make ourselves feel guilty, but to live in the truth. We're going to fail all the time, but let's at least admit we're failing instead of pointing the finger at other people and accusing *them* of failing.

I once went to Confession and mentioned, among other things, impure thoughts, and in the kindest, gentlest way, the old priest behind the grate said, "Yes, well, you know your body is the Temple of the Holy Spirit." . . . And you can laugh at that, and make fun of that all you want, but I, for one, have been stumbling and lurching around this desert for a long time now, trying to come to grips with my sexuality and sexual history, my longings, my capacity for love, my body—the fact that we even have bodies is strange almost beyond imagining—and where all of that stands with Christ. Because it couldn't possibly stand, any of it, anywhere else. And I don't understand it fully, and probably never will, except to know that somehow our bodies *are* Temples of the Holy Spirit—and that that is as sensible, reverential, helpful, and poetic a way to look at it as I, for one, can imagine. That's why we all feel it when, say, a child is defiled, especially by a person in a position of religious authority.

As for the Church, and all the other myriad complaints leveled against it: as much as I'd sometimes like to make it over a bit, I basically understand that the one who really needs to be made over is me. To that end, and I'm not bragging about it, I don't pay all that much attention to what goes on in the Vatican. I don't really care that women aren't allowed to be priests, for example; I just don't feel that constitutes some big lack in the Church, or that I'm being discounted or excluded. To my mind, it's not so much that we need women priests, it's that we need modern-day prophets and saints of every stripe: poets, painters, architects, musicians, teachers, waiters and waitresses, loan officers, child-care workers, contemplatives—"priests" of all kinds, any kind, who are excited about what they've found, who give the impression they're onto something and, in their possibly quiet way, are busting to tell about it. As for gays, maybe homosexuality isn't disordered but rather is ordered to a mystery the depths of which, when and if plumbed, will more fully illuminate *all* sexuality. In the meantime, I look to the Christlike virtues of patience, forbearance, humor, intelligence, and love with which my several gay Catholic friends attend Mass and otherwise participate in a Church that seems not to have yet quite found its bearings and balance in this area.

Also, in the meantime, if I'm really concerned about women or gays or any other minority being treated with love and respect, then I get to treat those people with love and respect myself, by doing all the hard, long inner work that treating any human being with love and respect inevitably entails. And in general that is exactly what the Church, more than any institution I know, urges and teaches: to treat *all* human life with love and respect, from the moment of conception to the dying gasp of the most diminished old age. The Church says I can't be against the murder of a family member but for the execution of the murderer; against the deaths of our eighteen-year-old soldiers and for the deaths of the other side's eighteen-year-old soldiers; for the starving child in Africa and against the one I'm carrying in my womb (or if I'm a guy, that I've fathered). More than any institution I know, the Church also tells me exactly where such a stance, for the very, very few who are brave and faithful enough to carry it out, leads. A religion that has as its central emblem its Head and Savior nailed to a cross, says, among other things, that when you practice real love, they'll kill you. If you tell the whole truth, eventually they'll kill you. Martin Luther King Jr. knew this. Gandhi knew it. More than anyone, Christ knew it.

Christ works in the individual human heart, and no institutional Church, whatever its strengths or defects, can ever change that. At the same time, he did establish a Church: proof positive that he was inviting his followers to participate in it. It's possibly the most thrilling moment in Scripture, the moment when Christ turns to Peter and says: "On this rock I will build my church, and the gates of Hades will not prevail against it" (Matthew 16:18). Part of the thrill lies in the sheer poetic audacity of the statement. Part is the assurance that, all evidence to the contrary, in the end the underdog—the weak, the fallen, the feeble, the poor in spirit—will triumph. And part of the thrill is that—unbelievably—he built it on one of us. Christ, the greatest creature who has ever walked or will ever walk the earth, entrusted his life's work to a simple fisherman who would betray him the night before he died, like we constantly do; raise himself up, just as we're capable of doing, and go on to be martyred himself, which people just like us have been called and risen to, day after imperfect day, ever since.

Refusing to become a Catholic because of the imperfections of the Church would be like refusing to donate to the Red Cross because a file clerk—or a disaster victim for that matter—might be siphoning off a little cash for his or her crack habit. I'd be wrong to claim the Church is perfect, but I'd be just as wrong to overlook the schools and orphanages and hospices, the faithful priests, the martyrs and saints, the incalculable amount of good, seen and unseen, that flows out from the Church, all over the world, and has for two thousand years.

As Flannery O'Connor observed in a letter to a nonbelieving friend, dated December 9, 1958:

To have the Church be what you want it to be would require the continuous miraculous meddling of God in human affairs, whereas it is our dignity that we are allowed more or less to get on with those graces that come through faith and the sacraments and which work through our human nature. God has chosen to operate in this manner. We can't understand this but we can't reject it without rejecting life.

The main reason we can't reject it without rejecting life is, again and always, the Eucharist. What distinguishes the Catholic Church utterly, finally, infinitely from any other church is that Christ left it as the repository of his Body and Blood, the Sacrament of Sacraments—pulsing, dynamic, eternal source of the power that created and rules over the universe—to nourish and connect us until the end of time.

Pope Benedict XVI tells a story of the early Christians:

In Abitene, a small village in present-day Tunisia, forty-nine Christians were taken by surprise one Sunday while they were celebrating the Eucharist, gathered in the house of Octavius Felix, thereby defying the imperial prohibitions. They were arrested and taken to Carthage to be interrogated by the proconsul Anulinus.

Significant among other things is the answer a certain Emeritus gave to the proconsul who asked him why on earth they had disobeyed the Emperor's severe orders. He replied: *"Sine dominico non possumus"*: that is, we cannot live without joining together on Sunday to celebrate the Eucharist. We would lack the strength to face our daily problems and not to succumb. . . .

Without Sunday, it is not possible for us. Without the Body and Blood of Christ—ground of all truth, justice, beauty, intelligence, knowledge, order, mystery—we wither and die. Without his ongoing, creative, ever-alive and eternal love for us—and ours for him—there is no order, no hope, no peace, no light, no life or possibility of life, no reason to go on.

If the Church's teachings on sex sound harsh, it may be good to remind myself that the Pope, cardinals, bishops, and priests have themselves offered up their entire beings—including their sexuality, by taking a lifelong vow of celibacy—to Christ. In fact, every Catholic, gay or straight, married or single, is called to chastity: each according to his or her own particular set of circumstances, each in his or her own way. One of the things I love about the Church is the incredibly wide latitude it affords in adhering to teachings that at first glance can look rigid or even impossible: the Church sets the highest possible standard, and then leaves the individual, in the full exercise of his or her freedom, to work things through. The Church doesn't pretend its teachings, on sex or otherwise, are going to be easy. It doesn't pretend trying to follow them isn't going to hurt. It doesn't pretend the struggle with sexuality isn't going to be a lifelong trial—but it's a lifelong trial, either way, for all of us.

I was talking on the phone recently to a fellow convert, my friend Ben in Madison, Wisconsin, who's lead singer/songwriter in a punk band and one of the most interesting and fervent Catholics I know. And he said, "You know, after we die we might find out the Church was wrong about some things. We might find out that divorce wasn't a grave offense, or that it was okay to have sex outside of marriage, or that homosexual acts weren't 'intrinsically disordered.' But for now, on earth, this is the highest guidance we have, the very best light we have to go by. If the Church was wrong, we will still have been obedient, and we, and the world, will have gained from our obedience, because it was from love."

After I hung up, I thought, *Yes, and no matter how high the standard the Church calls us to, if we rise to it, it can never* hurt *us.* We might lose out on pleasure, but never on joy. And that Sunday at Mass, I thought of something else. While I'm still scheming to carve out my own little loopholes in this area, somewhere, somehow, maybe in that Mass, maybe in some other Mass, there are men and women—divorced, single, married, gay—who are silently, anonymously doing the long, exacting work of consecrating their lives, including their sexuality, to Christ. While I'm still trying to take the low road, someone else is taking the very, very highest. The point of this is not to beat up on myself but to be humbled and instructed; to know that while I'm indulging myself in one way or another, someone else is refraining. And if they are indulging, they're refraining from taking the Eucharist, not out of guilt but out of a sense of honor and courtesy and reverence, because they themselves are willing to be humbled and instructed.

With all that, the Church seems to be undergoing a kind of slow, painful, perhaps much-needed death. "Unless a grain of wheat falls into the earth and dies, it remains just a single grain; but if it dies, it bears much fruit," Jesus said (John 12:24): maybe the Church is dying a little now so that it can bear its next crop of fruit. And the fact that so many of the issues involved are based on sex—birth control, abortion, gays, the ordination of female priests, celibacy, pedophilia—I can't help but think is a good thing. The area we all push into the netherworld of our subconscious, the last one we want to deal with because it is so painful, because it makes us feel so vulnerable, because there is such a huge gap between our longing for connection and our loneliness, because we're ashamed of our loneliness and think it's our fault, is the last area the Church perhaps has been fully willing to explore, too—the last area the Church has had the courage, heart, and tenderness to come fully to terms with, to reassess.

If anything can heal this wound, it's the Mystical Body of Christ. We need a new awareness of how closely we are connected, some new way of relating to each other, some dawning of a new consciousness that will enable us to cherish each other—man, woman, and child—as the precious, inviolate beings we are. Against the darkness and the loneliness. So at the moment of our deaths we can remember a gaze, a hand on ours, an embrace. A second when we weren't afraid.

I recently read of a documentary called *God Sleeps in Rwanda,* about five Tutsi women who survived the Hutu massacre. One had watched the Hutus butcher all seven of her children, been gang-raped so many times she'd lost count, and been left for dead, dumped in a local river. And then, almost in passing, the article about the film mentioned that she'd named her baby daughter—the result of one of the genocide rapes—Akimana: Child of God. And I thought, *Wait a minute, back up, back up.* She'd gotten pregnant by one of these butchers? She'd named it Child of God? She'd had the child? Assuming she'd had access to abortion, she even *had* the child? Later, I read more about her story and learned that the woman—Severa Mukakinia—in fact did have access to abortion, but after realizing the child was guiltless, decided to go ahead with the pregnancy.

In a country where, on the one hand, we'd have had the National Organization of Women (NOW), Planned Parenthood, and a banner-waving parade escort her to the abortion clinic, and on the other, a posse slavering to capture, try, incarcerate, and execute the rapist, this struck me as nothing short of revolutionary. This woman, who had next to nothing to begin with, who'd had every last thing taken from her, who'd been violated in so many ways—unspeakably violated, beyond imagination—still had something in her that wanted to give. Still had enough courage, strength, heart—whatever that would take, whatever word applies, if it exists—to bring a child into the world, to love the child, to name her Child of God. To pick herself up and stay standing and go on to give this new child a life, knowing full well she'd forever grieve the memory of her other seven. To do whatever unbelievable inner work she did to transform herself; to—again, for lack of a better word—forgive: to not hate the father so much that she had to hate his daughter as well, to let go of the terrible temptation to return violence with violence.

While the rest of us were debating the "solution" to genocide and crime and war, she had the baby. While we were casting the problems of the world as political issues, legal issues, or even "humanitarian" issues, she had the baby. That's the "answer" to genocide, crime, and war. That's the backward "triumph" of Christ who, when he said, "For truly I tell you, if you have faith the size of a mustard seed, you will say to this mountain, 'Move from here to there,' and it will move; and nothing will be impossible for you" (Matthew 17:20), must surely have been thinking of people like Severa Mukakinia—and of whom we should think, too, praying, just once before we die, to display a millionth of such faith, such duende, such balls ourselves. It's not the mightiest police force or the best-intentioned international tribune or even the most moving political speech that has the power to relegate all those countless acts of violence back to the realm of chaos where they belong: it's a single small human being, looking neither to the left nor the right, acting out of love. That's what restores order, sanity, a little corner of the Garden of Eden from which we are always ejecting ourselves.

In a 1939 lecture, Carl Jung (who, though not a Catholic, reflected deeply and fruitfully upon Christ) said that he was not concerned about the historic future at all. He was concerned only with those people who were going to "fulfill their hypotheses"—"to do today everything that is necessary so that my Father can rise over the horizon."

The Virgin Mary fulfilled her hypothesis. Severa Mukakinia fulfilled her hypothesis. And we have to, too, in the work we do, in the relationships we create, in deepening our capacity to love. So it is going to work out, somehow, and, we can hope, everywhere.

CHAPTER 6

Ho, everyone who thirsts,
　　come to the waters;
and you that have no money,
　　come, buy and eat!
Come, buy wine and milk
　　without money and without
　　price.
　　　　　—Isaiah 55:1

When I first converted, I made the mistake a lot of people do: I tried to be holy. In fact, I've always secretly wanted to be holy, a desire that, also unfortunately, has always been tied up with a very small pathological streak. When you think about it, actually, there's a very thin line between passion and pathology. Look at Jeffrey Dahmer: having sex with people, then killing and eating them. Okay, so he took it several steps too far, but haven't you ever wanted to devour someone? I know I have. The desire for physical, emotional, spiritual union, coupled with the fear of abandonment—well, killing the person is *one* way to get him or her to stay. Of course it's horrible beyond belief, but the point is that beneath all human pathologies is the craving for love, one way or another, gone awry.

If anybody knew about the thin line between passion and pathology, it was Jesus. That he left his Body and Blood to be eaten, in fact, is an echo of and answer to the hunger of Jeffrey Dahmer, which is to say the hunger of all mankind. And that the Mass is celebrated all over the world, every day, is a reflection of the fact that the hunger is never satisfied for good. Every day, we're hungry again; every day, we have to hold in balance the tension between passion and pathology; every day, we make a little progress in one area, only to find that, in another, we've regressed. "When the unclean spirit has gone out of a person, it wanders through waterless regions looking for a resting place, but it finds none. . . . Then it goes and brings along seven other spirits more evil than itself, and they enter and live there; and the last state of that person is worse than the first" (Matthew 12: 43–45). I'd already seen how, when I stopped using alcohol, I'd started using other things—sugar, caffeine, fantasy—to focus my anxiety, fill the void, numb my feelings. But one thing I was using I failed to see for a long time: the sick thrill of hoarding money.

For a long time I told myself I was being frugal—sacrificing for a higher cause—but, looking back, I was practicing something that was several degrees beyond frugality. In the early days of our marriage, for example, I periodically put Tim and me on what I called the AP: Austerity Program. Like the commandant of a concentration camp, I decreed that we eat turnips and cabbage, buy 99-cent-store shampoo, toothpaste, and reading glasses, and plan museum visits around the one day of the month—the third Wednesday, the second Thursday—when admission was free. I bought all my clothes, including shoes, at thrift shops, and that was *after* I started making good money as a lawyer. I declined all restaurant invitations on the theory that it was cheaper to eat at home; all movie invitations because it was cheaper to wait till they came out on video and rent them; and most travel unless it could be accomplished with a sleeping bag and a tent.

Converting to Catholicism brought part of me (the part that wanted to be free, to do God's will) into sanity and light, and plunged another part (the part that couldn't be free, that wanted to do my will and hide it under a seemingly noble motive) deeper into darkness. Since childhood, I'd been fascinated by Hetty Green, billed in the *Guinness Book of World Records* as the stingiest woman on earth. I'd joked about my fascination, but as an adult secretly strategizing to live on, say, eighteen cents a day, it wasn't turning out to be all that funny. Before quitting my job as a lawyer I'd saved up a nest egg, ostensibly to support myself while I wrote. This looked good on paper, except that I was so convinced that writing was my calling, that my mental/ emotional/spiritual health depended on being able to write, that the money I had at any given time was the only money I'd *ever* have, that protecting the nest egg rather than spending a penny of it quickly became a constant, borderline obsessive-compulsive preoccupation. I found enough freelance legal work to cover the bills and provide a teensy bit extra, and figuring out how to parlay that teensy bit extra into money for clothes, toiletries, entertainment, health care, and any number of other items turned into a full-time scheme/reason-for-living/job. It was amazing how much energy I could put into driving an hour each way for a five-dollar haircut, walking ten blocks to the Korean supermarket for free samples of dumplings, and punishing myself for getting a parking ticket by going without lunch for a week.

Such were the sacrifices, I told myself, I was willing to make for my art. And then I discovered the L.A. branch of the Catholic Worker, a lay movement started by Dorothy Day and Peter Maurin in the 1930s that espoused, among other things, acts of civil disobedience, workers' rights, and "voluntary poverty." "Voluntary poverty" was a concept guaranteed to cause my self-imposed pauperism to thrive, to validate my whole twisted attitude toward money, to prove I wasn't acting like a neurotic weirdo: I was in solidarity with Christ's poor.

I didn't stop to reflect that a soul as noble as Dorothy Day—and the courageous, deeply hospitable, profoundly kind folks at the L.A. Catholic Worker—could not possibly have been talking about a contest to see who could deprive themselves the most. I didn't stop to think that having $70,000 in mutual funds, working a part-time job that paid $90 an hour, and claiming, in any real sense of the word, to be poor was hypocritical at best and insane at worst. I didn't understand that for voluntary poverty to be a valid sacrifice, it had to come from a place of psychic, if not material, abundance. Instead, I took the fact that I squeezed myself in every morning between the mop bucket and the toolbox to write, that I hadn't treated myself to a new kitchen appliance in years (though I loved to cook), that I frequently worked myself into a state of nervous exhaustion as signs that I was willing to be a fool for Christ and thought, *Finally, FINALLY, I'm making some spiritual progress.*

It took me a long time to see that this wasn't holy, it was

masochistic; that it was based not on faith, but terror; that it presupposed a universe I had to cheat a little bit, to sneak around on, because if I did things the open, truthful way, there wouldn't be enough—money, food, love. I wasn't stingy with other people, just myself: I'd buy a $50 leather notebook for a friend's birthday but make my own notes in a chintzy spiral binder; on my one night off I'd visit another friend in the hospital instead of taking the rest I so badly needed. Sometimes the giving was from an open, generous heart, but just as often it was because I was afraid that if I didn't give a nice gift, or show up at the hospital, the person wouldn't like me anymore, thereby confirming I was the selfish, greedy, thoughtless person I'd always suspected myself to be.

So on I went, scavenging empty plastic bottles off the street and filling them with tap water; parking a mile away from the free chamber music concert rather than coughing up a couple of quarters to put in the meter. The folks who know say a bottom has to be reached with these things. My bottom came one spring morning. I'd driven up the coast to Oxnard (where someone had told me the rich people from Malibu carted their used stuff); pawed through the furniture, records, and clothes at the Retarded Citizens' Thrift Store for an hour or so; and repaired to the torn seat of my paint-peeling thirteen-year-old Mazda to wolf down the cold canned beans and barley with semi-rotting prosciutto I'd packed from home so I wouldn't have to shell out five bucks for lunch. Sitting in the hot sun, sipping the coffee with now-curdled milk I'd brought in a travel mug, the thought suddenly floated up from my subconscious: *something is really, really wrong.*

Luckily, help exists for people like me. I started talking to folks who were trying to bring some sanity to their money issues. They told me to start keeping track of every penny I earned and every penny I spent, because being specific with money—instead of eternally vague, as apparently many of us are—begins to remove some of the fear surrounding our relationship to it. They spoke of money not as some abstract, all-powerful, too-scary-to-come-into-contact-with higher being, but as an approachable, even friendly, tool. They posited the amazing idea that when repaying a debt, you were still supposed to go to the movies once in a while, or buy an occasional, say, $2.49 pint of raspberries. *Where was the martyrdom in that?* I wondered, harking back to the $35,000 student loan I'd paid off by living on Triscuits and moldy cheese for two years. Where was the control?

I met people who owed hundreds of thousands of dollars and I met millionaires who walked around with holes in their shoes, and underlying both extremes was the same failure of self-care with which I was so familiar, the same in my case self-defeating insistence on thinking of myself as too arty or intellectually evolved to work whatever job I had to in order to earn and spend enough money so I wasn't schlepping around with the clothes, car, and mind-set of a hobo.

I met someone who said that a debtor is someone who takes out of the world more than he puts back in, and, even though I didn't owe a penny, in that sense I was about as big a debtor as it was possible to be. It would have been one thing to build my life around free concerts and the discount produce bin at the grocery store if I were supporting my sick mother, or sending a kid to college; but my scrimping was all for me. And because it was all for me, I was creating my own private, ever more restricted and isolated hell. I was taking all my books out of the library and wondering why my own essays wouldn't sell. I was eating three-day-old salad for dinner and wondering why I always felt empty. It's one thing to avoid conspicuous consumerism, but I was refusing to put *any* money into the stream of commerce and then taking it as a sign of God's indifference that no matter how hard, and no matter with what grim determination I worked, none was flowing back.

I began to realize that the "powers and principalities" of the world aren't just out there in greedy corporations and nuclear weapons arsenals: they're inside me. When Christ said, "It is easier for a camel to go through the eye of a needle than for someone who is rich to enter the kingdom of God" (Matthew 19:24), he wasn't just talking about money: he was talking about a person's attachment to money. He was talking about a person's whole stance toward the universe; he was challenging us to examine our level of trust. The problem with not trusting is that it chokes up the channels to the riches of the universe that are flowing toward us every second, delighted at the prospect of lavishing themselves upon us. As long as we're focused on what we don't have, we're blinded to the incredible "wealth" that we do. I felt as if I'd been over in the corner all my life furtively clutching a morsel of dried bread, when in the other room, people were beckoning me to a banquet table laden with cornucopias of food. And I also had to look at the incredible amount of pride that lies beneath self-deprivation of any kind: the feeling of omnipotence that comes from living a secret life; the smug sense of superiority that came from telling myself I didn't need the things "normal" people did.

I knew from having gotten sober the difference between quitting and surrendering. When I'd stopped drinking, I never said I'm not going to drink again as long as I live. I said I'm just not going to drink *today*: maybe tomorrow, but I think I just won't have a drink today. So the solution to hoarding money wasn't to "make" myself stop hoarding money, it was to surrender my entire philosophy of, strategies toward, and capacity for earning, managing, and spending money to God.

This didn't happen all at once, or maybe I should say the way it did happen was so unplanned, so seemingly arbitrary, that it could easily not have happened at all. For years I'd been using the same printer, a behemoth Hewlett Packard Laser Jet II. It must have weighed 50 pounds, and though it did the job, all the while it had slowly become more obsolete, more unwieldy, more recalcitrant. The pages began to smudge on the back and blotch on the front. The front panel lights were busted. I am not a person who easily sees when something's no longer working. I like to believe things—appliances, relationships, my psyche— will miraculously fix themselves. So when the printer started to jam, first every ten pages, then five, then three, I chose to see it as a *temporary* malfunction. Every time it fed a page through, I waited with bated breath to see whether the rollers would engage. And when they didn't, I'd patiently pull out the tray, retrieve the errant piece of paper, push the tray back in, open the cover, blow off any stray toner dust, slam the cover down again, and push the reset button, all with such a delicately calibrated mixture of force, restraint, and prayer that I could have had a second career as a heart surgeon. Then the thing would jam again.

Most people have to stop spending money: I had to start. One Sunday morning, as what should have been a 15-minute printing job stretched to an hour, something snapped: it's *broken*, I realized. It's not *going* to get better. And that was when, in retrospect, something that was not "me"—or the me I'd been up to then—went into action. I consulted the yellow pages, found there are people who make Hewlett Packard house calls, 24/7, called one of them, and, an hour and a hundred bucks later, had a printer that actually worked. It doesn't sound like much, and if I'd been saner still, I probably would have just gone to Staples and bought a new one, but "letting go" in this tiny way—making the phone call, asking the question, spending the money instead of needlessly, neurotically suffering—changed my life.

It didn't change all at once, but I started to allow things that I'd been denying I needed—a decent tennis racket, good cookware—to enter my consciousness, and I began buying a few of them. The things themselves were nice enough, but what happened as a result was even nicer, and way stranger and more unexpected. I treated myself to a pedicure—my first ever—and soon after worked up the courage to look for my first-ever literary agent. I started going to a tax guy, found I'd been overpaying for years, and with the money I saved, went back for a longer-than-usual visit to my family in New England. I know this is going to sound like I made it up, but the week after I sold my crappy old car and bought a sporty Celica convertible, I came home and there was a message from an NPR producer, inviting me to write commentaries for *All Things Considered.*

It's been slow going, but I'm learning that in a sense I really do create my own universe. The idea isn't to get rich, obviously, though there's nothing wrong with that. The idea is to discover that if I act as if I'm worthy, worthy things will come to me—opportunities to meet people, give of myself, be of service—surely something of what Christ meant when he said, "A good measure, pressed down, shaken together, running over, will be put into your lap; for the measure you give will be the measure you get back" (Luke 6:38). The idea is to learn the discipline of self-examination, so that I'm not hiding a bad motive under a good one: greed under frugality, cruelty under honesty, lust under love. The idea is to realize that I can't be any more generous to other people than I am to myself.

I'll always have a tendency to hoard, but I no longer feel like the money I have now is the only money I'll ever have. I buy myself the things I need, for the most part, gratefully, and with confidence that if I do the footwork, more money will come in. I even give a little away now and then, not because I want people to like me, but because I want to, period.

At this rate, my financial guru will soon no longer be Hetty Green. It will be the poor widow (Mark 12:41–44) who, with the most open, trusting, and generous of hearts, gave her last two mites.

CHAPTER 7

I shall hear in heaven.

—Beethoven

It's a beautiful day in June, eight days before the day my father dies. I leave L.A. at six A.M., fly into Boston, and, in the waning light of late afternoon, drive north through the city, the suburbs, into the dense woods and rolling hills of southern New Hampshire. In an hour, I am pulling, with a complicated mixture of nostalgia and dread, into the driveway of my parents' house. The yard is usually as neat as a pin, but today the crab apple needs pruning, and it looks like the lawn hasn't been mowed in weeks.

I take in the kitchen at a glance: the blue cat dish by the radiator, the pot of ivy over the kitchen sink, my mother—plainspoken, dry-eyed—waiting to greet me. *Nothing's changed*, I think with relief as we hug. Then, over her shoulder, I spot the box of Depends, the walker, the IV pole huddled in the hallway, and the sight of these alien objects, invading the family abode like soldiers from an occupying army, takes my breath away. "Be prepared," everyone kept saying over the phone, "he's really gone downhill," but nothing has prepared me for this.

I turn back to Mom, my eyes a silent question, and she nods

toward the dining room. I take a deep breath and snake my head around the doorway. He's sitting in there, his back to me, in a wheelchair—a *wheelchair*. Nine months earlier, the last time I was home, we'd visited the Fuller Rose Garden, taken drives along the ocean down through Ipswich and Gloucester. Now his sticklike limbs swim inside paisley pajamas, and on his feet he wears Frankenstein shoes, outsize slippers of dark blue canvas with Velcro-fastened flaps.

I stand frozen for a minute, steel myself not to cry, and walk in. "Hi, Dad," I say softly. He turns his head—he turns his head so slowly now!—and when he lifts a liver-spotted hand and smoothes it back over his forehead, the hand moves too slowly, too.

For one terrible moment, I'm afraid he won't recognize me, but then he says weakly, "Hi, Heather." That's it. Not, How was your flight? or, At least you made it safe—the way he's said every other time I've come home in the last nine years. Just, Hi, Heather, as if I'd blown in from next door instead of 3,500 miles away. I sit down, put my arm around him, and press the side of my head against his. A little plastic plate of cut-up pieces of watermelon sits on the table before him.

"Are you hungry?" I ask.

His hand moves blindly for the fork.

Ever since the scare two years earlier at Christmas—we almost lost him then, but he rallied—my seven siblings and I have been on tenterhooks: calling each other, debating the best course to take, praying. Now he has kidney failure, congestive heart failure, diabetes, and blood circulation so poor that the ulcers he started getting on his feet nine months earlier have turned into full-bore gangrene. A recent vascular bypass operation not only almost killed him but also didn't work. The gangrene is inching up both legs, but he doesn't want them amputated and he probably wouldn't survive another surgery anyway.

Now the time for debate is past; now everyone's been notified; now we come home to sit vigil. Those of us who live farther afield drift in, one by one, during the next few days, and set up camp in our old bedrooms: Allen, Ross, and I from L.A.; Tim, back from Bangkok for the first time in nine years; Meddy, the baby, from western Massachusetts. The ones who live closer by, who have borne the brunt of the horror and grief of the last year, drive over every morning: Jeanne from the adjacent town of Greenland; Geordie the 17 miles from Eliot, Maine; Joe from Portsmouth, a few miles up the coast. All eight of us are together and accounted for, for the first time since anybody can remember.

In the living room, plastic basins of medical supplies occupy the space where the wooden rocker used to be, the couch has been pushed back to make room for the plastic commode. My father's world has shrunk to the distance between the hospital bed and the orange wing chair he sits in when he's not sitting in the wheelchair. We sit with him, not knowing at first it will be for a week—time in abeyance, normal life suspended—our existence reduced to eating, fitful sleeping, trips to the pharmacy, incessant phone calls, waiting, waiting, waiting.

In another life, we range in age from thirty-three to fifty-four; in another life, we have jobs, responsibilities, families of our own. Here, we are just our father's children again, vying for his attention, cracking jokes, telling stories to our all-time favorite audience. The air is thick with cries of Dad, Dad, Dad, a name we can't say enough because we know in a little while we will never have anyone to say it to again. Are you cold, Dad? Are you too hot, Dad? Daddy, how about a sip of ginger ale to wash down that pill? Hey, Dad, remember when we used to go out with you after work and pull lobster traps? How about that time we stayed in Bar Harbor and had a pajama party, that was a blast, wasn't it, Dad? Hey, remember that fat girl Dawn, that nurse last time you were in the hospital? What a jerk, huh, Dad?

He nods obligingly and echoes, "Yeah, what a jerk," and on his face is the shadow of a smile, as if he were remembering something that seemed funny a long time ago. When silence falls, he looks around at us, his eyes foolish with love, and says, "Well!" His feet are wrapped in white Kling bandages, perched like mummified egrets on his silver wheelchair rests, so tender he winces as soon as anyone gets within a yard of them. The big toe of his right foot is as black as charcoal, the nails of the others yellowed and retracting, the swollen skin seeping blood diluted with watery pus, like flesh that's been burned. Two, three, four times a day we call the doctor and beg him to up the dosage on the pain medication.

"I'm sorry it hurts so much, Dad. I wish I could do something so it wouldn't hurt," we tell him.

He squeezes his eyes shut, shifts his tailbone on the seat of the wheelchair, and whispers, "It's all right. Don't worry about that."

For the first few days he's restless: feeling for his glasses, fretting at his pocket for a Kleenex, shooting his wrist from his pajama cuff every other minute to look at his watch. He has a vague notion that since so many people are around he should be playing host, planning a party. At 7 A.M. he comes to and regards us blankly, as if we're strangers.

"Morning, Dad," Ross says, "and Joe and Heath are here, too."

"Oh," he replies. "How about if I take you all out to lunch?"

Fifteen minutes after we've eaten a huge dinner, "I've got an idea," he says.

"What, Dad? What?"

"How about having everyone over for fried clams, my treat?"

At 8 P.M., he gets a sudden burst of energy. "What are we doing now?" he fidgets. "Are we going out for a ride?"

"No, Dad, not now, it's almost time for bed. Aren't you tired, Daddy?"

"That would be nice," he sighs.

When we were kids, Dad showed us all how to fish for mackerel and dig clams. Geordie, a commercial fisherman, inherited my father's love for the water, and it's always been an almost sacred bond between them. After months of licensing snafus and bureaucratic tangles, just a few weeks earlier Geo had closed on his own 40-foot Bruno-Stillman. Nobody's been prouder or more excited over this turn of events than my father. Disoriented as he is, one phrase is still guaranteed to perk him up: "Geordie's boat."

"We're taking him out one more time if we have to carry him," Geo says bravely, so Saturday we bundle Dad up, prop him pygmy-style in the passenger's seat, and drive him up to Kittery. Geordie's made arrangements with the owner of a private pier that has a series of wheelchair-friendly ramps, and the boat's docked at Badger's Island, just over the Maine border. Tubs of pink petunias bank a fishing cottage of weathered gray shingles, and the air smells of creosote, but everyone's so emotionally overwrought it's hard to see the scene as picturesque. As Joe and Geordie push the wheelchair down to the *Seawitch*, Dad's head bobs gently; the rest of us trail behind with blankets, coolers, cameras. The "boys" discuss the logistics of getting him aboard while he gazes across the river to Portsmouth's waterfront: black-and-gold tugboats, brick warehouses.

"What a day, huh, Dad?" I say.

"Can't think of anyplace in the world I'd rather be," he quavers, raising a shaky hand to readjust his Red Sox cap.

Geordie and Joe hoist him over the railing and set up his wheelchair in the choicest spot they can find, an opening on the starboard edge.

"Where do you want to go, Dad," Joe asks, "out to sea or upriver?"

He thinks for a minute, then, with an odd glitter in his eye, points straight up, to the sky. We glance at each other. What is he saying: that he's ready to check out; that he wants to go to heaven? Upriver, we decide he means.

Geordie maneuvers us beneath the Piscataqua River bridge and we swarm around checking out the new boat: a snug cabin below, smelling of kerosene; a pale blue hold for the fish; coils of tarry rope. Back on deck, it's a perfect New England late spring day, the maples in full leaf, the clapboard houses gleaming with new paint, the greenswards of rich people's lawns, as green as golf courses, sloping down to the banks of the river. We take turns crouching beside Dad: hanging on to the back of his wheelchair, zipping and unzipping his jacket, offering him a sweater, a glass of juice, a bite of muffin, a pain pill. He lifts his face to the sun as the breeze riffles through what's left of his hair and, every so often, raises a trembling finger and points. He's down to one-word descriptions: "Pelican," he observes, or "Barge."

"Where's the *Seawitch*?" he wonders halfway through the trip.

"Uh, Dad?" I tell him gently. "We're *on* the *Seawitch*."

But it doesn't matter if he knows exactly where he is. He can smell the salt air. He can hear us as we surround him cracking our usual lame jokes. I wonder for a second whether we are doing this for him or whether he's doing it for us, but then I realize it doesn't really matter. Every few minutes, as if to reassure himself, his gaze strays toward the wheelhouse to drink in the sight he's dreamed of for so long: his son, Captain Geordie, at the helm of his own boat.

For the last eighteen months, my mother has been taking him in for dialysis—three days a week, four hours a day. The first Friday we're there, we drive him to the center for his usual treatment, but it's awful. Anyone who's been in a similar situation knows it raises all kinds of thorny questions. Could it possibly contribute to a dying man's dignity to prop him up in a chair for four hours, slowly drain every drop of blood from his body, and then slowly pump new blood back in? Is it compassion to keep a person alive for another week or two just because, with modern medicine's sometimes violent, invasive procedures, you can? What does it mean to die with dignity, anyway? The very question prompts me to look up "dignity" in our old *Webster's* and find it's from the Latin *dignitas,* meaning "worth" or "merit." In that case, isn't it impossible to die *without* dignity? In God's eyes, don't we all have merit, no matter what kind of shape we're in? I wanted to remember my father when he was vibrant, coherent, pleasing to look at and listen to. But while it wasn't working out that way, it had never been clearer that I loved him not because of what he could do, know, or understand—but because he existed at all.

One of our health-care system's other delightful mores is that the excruciating pain of one's last days—the man's legs are rotting—is to be preferred over the hideous prospect of becoming a doomed-to-die-anyway drug addict. He's eligible for at-home hospice care—one of the major benefits of hospice being that they're allowed to bring on the pain meds full bore—but the catch-22 is that he can't get hospice care as long as he's still undergoing a "life-sustaining" measure such as dialysis. So over the weekend we have a series of family powwows. We talk to the people at the dialysis center, who say he's so weak he might not survive another treatment; we arrange to go to the hospital; we crowd around the conference table while his doctor confirms that there's no hope, either way, and explains that without dialysis, he'll probably go into a coma and die within a week. As it is, he's becoming more incoherent by the hour. Monday morning we make the decision not to bring him in again; it's the most wrenching thing any of us has ever done. The good news is we're able to call the insurance company and immediately switch over to hospice. Right away, the nurse gets him a prescription for morphine patches.

We run to the drugstore to fill it, run back, paste one, pale as a communion wafer, to his chest. Within minutes, he seems to rest a little easier.

All day long the screen door bangs open and people from our past come through, bearing gifts, like Magi. Our longtime next-door neighbor Vicki Fish, at eighty-three, still wearing dangly earrings, diamond rings, and gold lamé flats, brings two perfectly roasted chickens. Mrs. Luff, Meddy's old friend Alex's mother, brings peonies cut from her garden. Joe the Barber brings his little brown bag, drapes a towel around Dad's neck, and gives him a trim. My old friends the Cushings come: Marynia with a shepherd's pie, Janet with a fruit basket. Dick and Diane Jones, our neighbors from forty years earlier, drop off a pan of ravioli; Nellie Richards, whose kids Jerry and David I used to babysit, leaves a raspberry coffee cake; Freddie Pridham—he and my father, both bricklayers, worked weekends together for years—arrives with a loaf of stone-ground bread.

After a few days, we get the bright idea to start rating people's offerings: ten for homemade veal parmigiana, five for store-bought muffins, two for the cheapskates who come empty-handed. This is quintessential Dad humor, used to hide emotion: pretending not to be grateful when you are really so grateful you could cry. In fact we are moved to incoherence by this outpouring of support, stunned by the affection our father has engendered in his friends. At seventy, Freddie Pridham is still built like an ox with a mouthful of big, blindingly white teeth, a chest like the prow of a ship, and mammoth arms forested with hair. He looks like an ax wouldn't fell him, but after he visits with my father, we say good-bye and watch him stagger out to his pickup, lean against the door, and collapse, sobbing. We hold half-hour phone conversations with relatives of my mother's we've never met, we catch up with people we haven't seen in twenty years, we lean against the kitchen counters to drink in familiar faces grown weathered by age, everyone with their kind words, their reassuring hugs that smell of windblown laundry, their own stories of loss: the daughter gone to leukemia, the brother to a stroke, the grandmother who was two months in a coma.

In the end, they all say the same thing: *you never stop missing them.*

I begin to understand that cliché about the resemblance between old people and babies. Life reduced to bright colors, basic concepts: hungry, thirsty, do you have to go to the bathroom? Talking loudly when people come over to visit, as if that will help: It's ARCHIE MCKINNON, Dad. You remember MRS. BASSETT, don't you? Watching the treacherous progress of a spoonful of ice cream as it makes its way from the bowl to his small, birdlike mouth.

And also as if he were a baby, I have some primal urge to touch him: to run a comb through his thinning hair, swab his mouth with a sponge, feel his breath on the back of my hand as I feed him a pill. It's the sacrament of flesh, this making contact, as intimate as sex, or the intimacy we long for and so seldom reach in sex. When he can't stand up anymore, my sister Jeanne, a nurse, teaches us how to pair up and form a human chair by gripping forearms across his back and opposite forearms under his knees: "Put your arms around our necks, Dad, that's right, watch your shunt, one, two, three, lift—DON'T HURT HIS FEET!—pivot, easy, *easy*, push the commode *this* way, Mom." I feel a rivulet of sweat run down my back, not because my father is heavy but because he's so light it's scary. We set him down like a rag doll, pajama pants around his ankles, his worn face startled and set, like the only survivor of a plane crash.

With all that, he never succumbs to despair. Every so often, he'll snap out of a doze, gaze around at whoever happens to be hanging around his chair, and sigh in his New England accent, "Ahn't I fohtunate, having you all home like this." Mom putters around in the background cooking, cleaning, letting us have our day with the old man. She corroborates how much it means to him that we're here. "It's all he talks about," she says. "Every time we're alone he looks at me and says, 'We're awfully lucky to have such nice kids.'"

Having never been exactly what you'd call a demonstrative family, we bask in this reflected warmth, emboldened to let out all the stops. We have always depended on him, but now he is gripping *our* hands, grabbing *our* shoulders, accepting *our* help. The effect is transformative. We, who tend to communicate by ridicule, are blurting out, "I love you, Dad"—right in front of everyone. We, who in childhood came to fisticuffs over whether we were going to watch *Green Acres* or *The Beverly Hillbillies*, are coming together to lock arms and carry our father to bed. We, who have always prided ourselves on our sarcasm, are reporting back to each other on his every word and move, in voices hushed with reverence. When we look at each other, tears flow so spontaneously it's like breathing: after a while, we don't even bother to wipe them away anymore.

My husband, Tim, now officially also a nurse, takes a few vacation days from his job at L.A. County Hospital and flies out to help. Some people are good with children or dogs: he, we all see immediately, is good with sick people, lifting and turning and talking to Dad with just the right combination of authority and gentleness. Desperate for a reprieve, we instantly appoint him liaison to the cavalcade of doctors, pharmacists, and nurses who march across the landscape of our days.

But even Tim sometimes strikes out. "If one is no pain at all and ten is the worst pain you can imagine, where on the scale are you, Al?" he asks.

"That's true," my father replies.

The two of us dose him with Oxy-IR, give him a Restoril, prop him up on his wing chair—he prefers his chair to the hospital bed, we think because when his feet are hanging down they hurt less—and sleep on the pull-out couch beside him. A pilled pink blanket bunched over our sweating bodies, my father breathing raggedly beside us, I curl into Tim's warm, familiar body and fall asleep thinking, *This is the sacrament. This is what marriage is really about.*

Tuesday morning I wake at five, dress, and drive down Atlantic Avenue the four miles to Ocean Boulevard. Rhododendrons bloom, mist rises from open fields, and fanned out along the ocean are the summer "cottages" of wealthy folks from Massachusetts, with their sweeping picture windows and colonnaded porches and empty lawns. I walk along the boardwalk, fine needles of salt spray cooling my face. Beach plums are alive with deep pink roses; the stone walls bordering the mansions blaze with hollyhocks and foxglove. It is a scene—and time of day— my father, both of us early risers, would have loved. Brown seaweed spreads itself out like hair over the barnacled rocks; gulls send up plaintive cries. Waves lap in with a tongue of foam and recede, the smooth weathered rocks clattering like bones.

By Wednesday, he is starting to hallucinate. In the hospital bed, his hand strays again and again to the guardrail, as if groping for a phantom limb. "Can we take this down?" he pleads. "I won't fall out of the car."

His eyes are stricken, wild: "The lawnmower's wet!" he bursts out. "Watch out, Jeanne, there's something sticking out of the floor!" "I see a head!" "Whose head?" Meddy asks. "It's Janet," he says. Janet is our mother.

He's had false teeth since he was thirty, but this is supposed to be a big secret: none of us have ever seen him without his teeth. That afternoon four or five of us are hanging out, as usual, and Dad is sitting in his chair, staring fixedly into the cold fireplace.

"I was thinking . . .," he says. We all lean forward but he trails off, his finger pointing at some invisible spot in an invisible dimension, the thought dissolved in the ether, unfurling, if at all, light-years away. And then he very calmly opens his mouth, reaches in with both hands, and extracts his dentures. It's like that scene at the end of Koestler's *Darkness at Noon* where

Rubashov drops his glasses, hesitates for a moment, then, realizing he won't be needing them anymore, gropes the rest of his way to the firing squad. After a while Allen, my oldest brother and my father's namesake, stands up, walks over, and gently takes the teeth from my father's hand.

It's been six days since his last dialysis treatment, but, on Thursday morning, amazingly, he still recognizes us. "Hi, Ross," he says in a faraway voice. "Hi, Jeanne." The hospice nurse tells us she thinks he's "holding on" for some reason and suggests we go in, one by one, and tell him it's all right to "let go." A week earlier, the thought of sitting down beside my father and telling him it was okay to die would have been unthinkable. Now, it simply seems like the next indicated thing to do in this reality-suspended time. *We'll take care of Mom*, we tell him. *You're the best father in the world and you always will be. Everything's going to be all right.*

Tim has to get back to L.A., and that afternoon Meddy and I drive him to the airport. When we return, Mom, Jeanne, Ross, Allen, and my brother Tim are all gathered around his chair in the living room.

"Look at the skin over his cheekbones, how tight it is," Mom says.

It's true. In the space of just a few hours, he's faded: he looks like a bouquet of flowers kept a few days too long. His skull seems to be pushing out from the inside, stretching the skin taut and deepening the hollows of his eyes. His mouth is slightly open, his tongue is curled, and he is breathing deeply with long intervals in between: Cheynes-Stokes breathing, Jeanne tells us; a sign the end is near.

Allen is holding his left hand; I sit down on the piano bench and take his right. We watch him in silence, inhaling and exhaling along with him, our bodies in communion. Someone says we should call Joe and Geordie, and someone does: they are on their way down from Portsmouth.

He takes a deep, ragged breath and winces. "Okay, Daddy," Med whispers.

A few minutes later, he takes another breath, lets it out—and then he doesn't breathe anymore. We sit in silence for what seems like an eternity. Finally, I tear my eyes away and look down at my brothers and sisters and mother. Their faces are white.

Jeanne gets her stethoscope, snakes it down the front of his pajama top, listens for a second or two. "It's all over," she says, and with some elemental instinct, we form a circle, join hands with his, and begin: "Our Father, who art in Heaven . . ."

That night I slept in his bed, the hospital bed we'd set up in the living room, the one on which my brothers laid him out to bathe before the men came from Remick Brothers. Watching the hearse back down the driveway and onto Post Road—the last time my father would leave this house he'd built, the house he'd fathered some of us in—I found my right hand going up to lay itself over my heart. I'd seen photos of firemen, their hats laid over their hearts for a fallen comrade, but I'd never known it's instinctive: not only the making of a final salute, but a gesture buried deep within us, to let the person know our souls are bound to theirs, forever.

I could have slept in another bed that night, or made his up fresh, but I didn't want to: I wanted to be as close to him as I could, one last time. Lying there on the pale orange sheets, spotted lightly from my father's wounds, I knew that we are loved absolutely, that suffering is collective, that, like Christ, my father had somehow died for all of us. We want to hide death, we're afraid of death, but it has so much to teach us.

We took a lot of photos that morning on Geordie's boat. One in particular grips my heart. It is a picture of my father, his head framed by the pale green river behind him, his shoulders stiff with pain, his hand clutching a thigh. Half of his face is in shadow, the eye drooping closed; the other eye is wide open to the light, a fixed, blank look to it, as if it were staring into a world way beyond this one. His expression is a mixture of terror and the dawn of an awful peace—as if, on the far far horizon, he was just beginning to glimpse what it might mean to have borne his suffering to the last drop.

I have no way of knowing what that means myself, no proof that the last will be first, that the meek will inherit the earth, that the poor shall enter the kingdom of heaven. I only know that I have looked at the face in that photo so many times, I no longer see just my father. I see myself. I see my mother and my brothers and my sisters. And every so often—on a good day—I am even starting to see you.

CHAPTER 8

Prayer arises, if at all, from incompetence. Otherwise there is no need for it.

—St. Thérèse of Lisieux

If you have any kind of hermit leanings, as I do, becoming a Catholic offers all kinds of inviting opportunities. One of them is making retreats at monasteries or convents—not that you have to be a Catholic for that. Whatever the case, I returned to L.A. from New Hampshire shell-shocked from my father's last days, his funeral, the nervous strain of spending two weeks cooped up with my brothers and sisters in the house where we were raised. It seemed like extragood timing that I was scheduled, shortly after my return, to make a five-day retreat at a monastery about an hour outside L.A. called St. Andrew's Abbey.

Unfortunately, in the intervening week I went hiking in the Santa Monica Mountains and contracted a virulent case of poison oak. I looked like a leper; people averted their eyes when I wore shorts. At night I rose every hour to bathe my welt-covered legs with ice chips, dust them with baby powder, and lie back down, praying for sleep. I almost canceled, but I'd been looking forward to the retreat for months and I badly needed to get away. So in the end, I got up that morning, draped blue ice-gel packs over my burning shins, and drove the Angeles Forest highway to Valyermo, a tiny town on the edge of the Mojave Desert.

In spite of my affliction, the monastery was like balm to my troubled soul. The hills shimmered gold and green, the air smelled of sweet grass, and the Divine Office (a special order of prayers observed by the monks) lent a soothing rhythm to the day: Vigils at 6, Lauds at 8, Vespers at 6, Compline at 8:30. (Mass was at noon.) I woke before dawn and sat on the stone patio, watching rabbits creep through stands of artemisia as the sun rose. I sat for hours in the garden, listening to the breeze soughing through the tops of Lombardy poplars. After dinner, I climbed the hill behind the duck pond to the cemetery, with its rows of plain stone crosses, and watched the sun set. At the end of Compline, just before we went our separate ways in the dark, the abbot intoned, "May the all-powerful Lord grant you a restful night and a peaceful death," and sprinkled us with holy water. Then the Great Silence began, which lasted until after breakfast the next morning.

When the itching became unbearable, I lay in the dark and thought about my father's death. Could you call that peaceful? I wondered. It was peaceful the moment he died, but that's always peaceful. What about what went before? How much had he known of what was happening? What had gone through his head? Remembering his blackened toenails and swollen, weeping flesh, I wondered if my poison oak constituted a kind of sympathetic pain, as if, unable to save my father in life, I was determined to suffer with him in death.

Back home in L.A., I thought of all the beautiful places in the world: the Sonoran Desert, the hills of Crete. Instead, for eight years now I had lived in a noisy, crime-ridden ghetto where people left their burnt-out refrigerators on the sidewalk, where no sooner did the city plant a tree than the neighborhood children chopped it down with machetes.

True, our gem of a garden courtyard apartment was dirt cheap; and, on my better days, I loved the manic energy, the chaos, the fact that I was never more than a few steps from a pupusa stand, a Korean barbecue, or a four-dollar bowl of pho. Still, it occurred to me that I had lived in a variation of this apartment my entire adult life. I had always considered myself a kind of cutting-edge urban warrior, daring and cross-cultural for immersing myself in such neighborhoods. After yet another night punctuated by periodic blasts of ranchera music, however, I was feeling less cross-cultural than at cross-purposes, and as for the otherwise adorable Korean kids next door, the fact that they spent their days running up and down the porch and shrieking was enough to bring one word to mind: AK-47.

I was too old for this: I realized I was forty-seven, it was time to grow up. So I bought the *Recycler*, made dozens of phone calls, and even, against my better judgment, joined an online rental agency; but now that I was ready to grow up, it turned out there were no decent apartments anywhere, not in Hollywood or Echo Park or Silverlake, not in Los Feliz or Melrose. I must have looked at thirty different places and they all reeked of cat piss or had a playground next door or were a variation of the same depressing '60s complex: blinds, carpeting, musty A/C.

I combed the classifieds, I put out the call to everyone I knew, I even took to cruising the streets, looking for "For Rent" signs. I lay in bed at night sweating, listening to the crackheads pushing their shopping carts up and down the alley, thinking, *How did I get here? What if I never get out?*

My only comfort came from praying, or rather attempting to pray, the Liturgy of the Hours, the way the monks had on retreat. It was at a previous retreat that I'd first learned of the Liturgy of the Hours, also known as the Divine Office: the Psalms, readings, and canticles from both the Old and New Testaments, recognized by the Catholic Church as a special form of prayer. Until then I'd never known that anyone after about 50 A.D. even remembered what the Psalms were. As it turned out, saint after saint, contemplative mystic after contemplative mystic, not to mention Christ himself, had found these ancient poems to be a channel to the love of God. In the Divine Office, monks and nuns prayed them, felt them, experienced them, chanted them together at four or five set times during the day, year in, year out, until lines like "My heart is in anguish within me, the terrors of death have fallen upon me" (Psalm 55) or "The voice of the Lord causes the oaks to whirl, and strips the forest bare; and in his temple all say, 'Glory!'" (Psalm 29) were branded on their hearts and brains.

The Second Vatican Council had emphasized that the Divine Office should be the prayer of laypeople as well as of priests, monks, and nuns. So I'd been dabbling in it for a while, at least praying the Morning Prayer, and often Evening or Night as well. But this time on retreat, in the quiet of the blue-shrouded hills of Valyermo, I'd sensed the possibility of a whole new way of being: I'd felt, or understood a bit, how prayer in general, and the Divine Office in particular, could be used as a way of consecrating time, ordering one's day, seeking God's will. The fidelity of the monks who gathered morning, noon, and night in the chapel to pray, the power of the Psalms that so majestically encompassed the spectrum of the human condition: all this reverberated, prompted me, however falteringly, to grope a little further into the darkness of prayer.

Perhaps I should say that I am not, at first glance, a person in any way cut out for prayer. I'm nervous, jumpy, easily distracted, and my mind tends to run in obsessive ruts—usually on subjects that are far removed from prayer. So at first, developing a prayer life sounded way too advanced and esoteric for me. But then I came across a quote from Dom John Chapman, a twentieth-century British priest, monk, and biblical scholar, who said, "Pray as you can and do not try to pray as you can't. Take yourself as you find yourself; start from that."

Personally, I wanted to start with St. John of the Cross and go straight to the "living flame" of infused contemplation, but I saw that for someone who couldn't get through "Now I lay me down to sleep" without several time-outs to mull over resentments, descend into sexual reverie, or wonder whether I could buy almond paste at Ralphs or if I would have to go to Vons— shoot, I was up on Melrose today, I could have stopped in at Pavilions—this was unlikely. In a way I didn't feel *worthy* to pray the Psalms, but if they were for laypeople, that meant they were even for jumpy, easily distracted laypeople. I had to remind myself I wasn't after some exalted state; I wasn't trying to have an "experience." I just wanted to know myself a little better, do a little better when it came to loving my fellow man. I just wanted to get closer to Jesus.

Of course my apartment wasn't quite like the abbey at

Valyermo, with its incense and stained glass and lilting harp, the monks chanting their Psalms in the midst of respectful, peaceful silence. At around six one morning, I was just settling onto the sofa with my breviary when someone pulled up out front and proceeded to lay on the horn—HOOONNK, HOOONNK, HOOONNK—what in these parts we refer to as a "Mexican doorbell."

"Shut up, you CRETIN!" I screamed out the window, then slammed back onto the sofa cushions, made the sign of the cross over my mouth, and hissed, "Lord, open my lips, and my mouth shall proclaim your praise."

I realized this was not the optimal frame of mind in which to approach God, but I was too emotionally drained to pretend I was nicer or more tolerant than I actually was. Oddly enough, my defects were precisely why, as I continued in my bumbling but semiregular way, day after day, week after week, the Psalms resonated within me so deeply. The passages of praise were of unparalleled beauty, but it was the Psalms of lamentation—their descriptions of the backbreaking burdens and crushing struggles and dark nights of the soul we go through on the way to the praise—that really spoke to my heart. Nothing I was reading in *The New Yorker* or *Harper's* that summer seemed even remotely as relevant as a passage like this:

> *From day to night you bring me*
> *to an end;*
> *I cry for help until morning;*
> *like a lion he breaks all my bones;*
> *from day to night you bring me*
> *to an end.* (Isaiah 38:12–13)

I myself was struggling financially (if at least no longer hoarding), but everyone I knew seemed to have gotten rich. I'd talk to my friends back East and they'd say, "Oh, I was just walking my Irish wolfhounds down by the trout stream," or "Oh, I went to see a play about Sarah Orne Jewett on the grounds of an old colonial house by the ocean last night," or "Can you hold on a minute, the deer are in the apple trees again." My college roommate sent me a postcard with a stunning aerial view of sapphire blue water and a wooded island and wrote on the back, "We found our dream house in Vermont, 400 feet of lakefront property, e-mail me!" I e-mailed her, congratulating her on her good fortune, but she never answered.

Meanwhile, I was holed up in my sweltering apartment, trying to write through the sound of whining helicopters, blaring car alarms, barking rottweilers, horse-powered leaf blowers, honking horns, and the demands and remarks of a husband who seemed to think writing was a kind of hobby, something I did for *fun*. I began to picture myself at eighty, stuck in some shabby convalescent home up on Hollywood Boulevard, shuffling up and down the sidewalk in a ratty chenille bathrobe. I'd be smoking Pall Malls (I'd quit years earlier but would have taken it up again out of boredom and desperation), my fingers yellow with nicotine stains, my teeth like old piano keys, barking, "Move it, Sonny!" to the leather-jacketed youths who dared to cross my path. Or worse, I'd be bumming cigarettes from them, putting on a little vaudeville act, playing the buffoon.

There was a time when I would have chalked my situation up to bad luck, but I knew better now: clearly my old friends had the right temperament for joy and success and I did not. I could have put roots down like they had, but no: as usual, I'd been restless, irritable, discontent; the winters had depressed me (What didn't? I wondered now); I'd had to move somewhere glamorous and stimulating where my genius would be recognized, somewhere like L.A., where my writing "career" was bringing in about five grand a year and there was apparently not a single affordable, halfway-quiet two-bedroom apartment in the entire city that wasn't located in the crosshairs of a gang war.

And now, as I looked at apartment after apartment, rejecting each one in turn for being too small, too ticky-tacky, too expensive, I started to wonder if it wasn't the apartments that were "wrong," but me. Was I being picky because deep down I was *afraid* to move? Why did the simplest decisions overwhelm me? Was I destined to wander the earth without ever finding a true home?

> *My dwelling is plucked up and*
> *removed from me*
> *like a shepherd's tent;*
> *like a weaver I have rolled up my*
> *life;*
> *he cuts me off from the loom.* (Isaiah 38:12)

By August, my apartment search had still borne no fruit. "It's already been rented," the person snapped if I was lucky enough to reach an actual human being: 95 percent of the time I left messages which nobody bothered to answer. I began to suspect that "people of color" were discriminating against me because I was white: even paranoid people have enemies, I told Tim, and I was only half-kidding. I had always regarded my neighbors with a mixture of amusement, irritation, and affection, but now my feelings had an edge I found frightening. They had become doppelgängers for my inner demons, enemies who were persecuting me, assaulting me, "compassing me about," as the psalmists described it. I felt caged in a way I never had before in L.A.—even the palm trees looked menacing—and full of unfamiliar anger.

All my life I had subconsciously assumed I would do better than my parents: be wiser, make more effective decisions, live longer. But searching in vain that summer for an apartment where I could lead a perfect—or at least different—life, I saw for the first time that there was a limit to what I was going to accomplish on earth, that even the most fervent prayer wouldn't make things go my way, that life is a series of losses and in the end, I would die, too.

"Why don't you go back to *Jalisco!*" I found myself screaming out the window one afternoon at a *paleta* vendor who'd been honking his bicycle horn for the last hour, and burst into tears. I didn't know whom I felt worse for, the ice cream vendor toiling in the hot sun, my father, or me, but that was when I realized the path to God is way longer, rockier, and harder than I'd ever imagined.

> *Like a swallow or a crane I*
> *   clamor,*
> *I moan like a dove.*
> *My eyes are weary with looking*
> *   upward.*
> *O Lord, I am oppressed; be my*
> *   security!* (Isaiah 38:14)

At dusk I lie in bed and gaze out my bedroom window, through the bamboo blinds, at the backs of the apartment buildings across the way. As the sky beyond begins to darken, I imagine my neighbors all lying in their beds, too, gazing at the same sky. I imagine the air thickening with our memories: memories of Mexican beaches, Korean mountains, Salvadorean rain forests, and, from my bed, almost crowded out by the hundreds of other beds in this single block, the memory of the weeping willow I could see from my bedroom window all through my childhood, in the house where I dreamed of growing up and moving on to some other, better place of living happily ever after.

If religion is consolation, as the atheists sneer (and why any human being would begrudge another a moment of consolation is beyond me), why isn't there more of it? What is the sorrow of this human condition where we always yearn to be somewhere we're not, where every birth contains a death, every reunion a parting, where happiness seems eternally just beyond our reach? As the sun sets in a wash of red, beyond the telephone poles and obscuring rooflines, I wonder: *Does it really matter where I live? Is any place quiet or beautiful enough to deliver me from the exile of my own limitations? Where is the apartment, the city, the kingdom that will free me from this terror and doubt?* That is not the kind of answer I've found thus far in prayer, but all I know is to keep praying, in the midst of the doubt. Because prayer has brought me one thing, and that is to know that everybody feels this way. We're all in exile. We're all on a long, solo desert journey.

"Oh, that you may suck fully of the milk of her comfort," the prophet Isaiah wrote of Jerusalem, the promised land, "that you may nurse with delight at her abundant breasts" (Isaiah 66:11). Down in the alley someone cranks up a boom box. For a second, I stiffen instinctively with rage. Then the strains of a Mexican lullaby, all muted horns, drift out and settle over the block like a well-worn blanket, as if we were brothers and sisters in some huge, lost family; as if an invisible father were smoothing our brows, inviting us to rest.

CHAPTER 9

Our enemy is not somebody far off in a distant land. Our enemy is somebody close by who threatens us, who blocks us.

—Jean Vanier, founder of L'Arche, a movement of faith communities where people with developmental disabilities live along, and share life, with their caretakers

I tend to think of myself as easy to get along with. *I never have fights with people,* I used to think. But it's slowly dawning on me that I have fights with people all the time. I once stopped speaking to my brother Allen for two years (I don't think he even noticed) because he criticized the way I held my chopsticks. I once stopped playing tennis for a year with my partner Rachelle over a poor sportsmanship snafu. Then there's my little sister Meredith (Meddy). Meddy lives in the Berkshires, writes songs, and, like all my siblings, is good, kind, and really, really funny.

One year on my annual visit home, for example, Meddy and I were visiting with our cousin Patty and her husband, Dick.

"What are you up to, Meredith?" Dick asked when we'd settled in.

"Oh, looking for a place to live," she said.

"Wonderful!" he boomed. "What's the price of real estate out your way?"

"I—I'm not sure," she stammered.

"*Real estate?*" she whispered when he left the room a minute later. "I was thinking more along the lines of maybe a *tent.*"

So Meddy's funny, self-deprecating, and good, but she also sometimes says things that hurt my feelings. Several years ago, on another visit, for example, she commented upon the tone I took with our mother when discussing whose bedroom I would stay in; another time she very unkindly insinuated I had a pot belly. But we'd never had a major fight till a few years ago, when she asked to borrow some money. Actually, she didn't *ask* to borrow some money; she said she'd had a resentment against me for months because she'd been telling me how poor she was and I hadn't offered to *give* her any money.

Now as I've said, I had "issues" around money, and I'd done a lot of inner work—inventory writing, consulting with my peers, praying—trying to deal with them. I was spending more in general and though I'd also started to be more generous in giving a little money away here and there—twenty bucks each Sunday at church, an extra few bucks to the homeless—I wasn't quite ready to extend this in any regular way to a family member. I had all kinds of emotional baggage to contend with: my oldest-child-syndrome tendency to be overresponsible, my determination not to repeat my parents' mistake of taking on other people's burdens while neglecting themselves. For years, I'd been sending Meddy $25, $35, $50 on her birthday and for Christmas. Where was the acknowledgment of the money I'd given *already*? I wondered now. I had more money than my sister, true, but did that mean I was obligated to share any of it with her—especially in light of the fact that my actual income at that point wasn't much above poverty level? The words of Cain rang in my ears: Am I my brother's keeper? On the other hand, well, *aren't* we our brothers' and sisters' keepers? Aren't we everyone's keeper? Who else will keep our brothers and sisters if not us?

So I was torn—on the one hand wanting to do the right thing, on the other not wanting to do something I was uncomfortable with just because I was afraid to say no. What if I said no and she turned on me? What if I said no and she went to my mother, who could afford it even less than I but never said no to anything? What if I said no and *she killed herself*? It was the type of situation that triggered all the parts of me I kept most deeply buried: my terror of confrontation, my tendency to be passive-aggressive rather than honest, the whole dark seething brew of guilt, shame, fear, and self-deprivation I hadn't quite worked through (do any of us ever work it totally through?) with my family.

At any rate, momentarily forgetting the wonderful maxim that "no" is a complete answer—and out of what I felt to be the incredible, and usual, kindness of my heart—I e-mailed that I wouldn't feel comfortable giving her money, and, as best I could, explained why. As gently as possible, I said I felt it was my choice and that maybe I was wrong but I was willing to suffer the consequences; that I had my own fear of codependency, money, and self-care issues to contend with (for instance, while I didn't have health insurance at the time, my sister did); that I felt I had to draw this boundary in order to be free to be loving—i. e., free of resentment, etc., and therefore present and open—in the larger sense.

My journal entry for the next day read, in part:

And when I got home last night, she'd sent really this extraordinary e-mail. I've never received anything like it, this overweeningly patronizing missive about how I really might want to seek help because obviously I am in some kind of sickness that is not normal, and a prisoner, and how of course I can do what I want with my money but it just seems *odd* that I wouldn't want to help and she hopes I can get help because though it is indeed scary maybe I could then have the courage to face who I am. . . . Really, it was unbelievable, not least because of the complete and utter lack of compassion. As it is, I have fully copped to having money issues—I've opened up to her about them, just as she's opened up to me about her stuff—and instead of being understanding, she was all *shaming*. She was using the things I'd told her in confidence against me! I'm not naturally generous, it's true, but is it all that courteous of my sister to bring it to my attention? And this whole time when I've been trying to be understanding and supportive and fair and keep an open heart and falling all over myself to go to the Berkshires every summer and visit, she has not had my well-being in mind at all! I was literally shaking as I read it and shot back an e-mail saying she'd been entirely free to ask and I'd been entirely free to say no, and that her "opinions" were completely unsolicited and uncalled for, and that I felt completely unsafe talking to or sharing anything with her and did not want to communicate further. . . .

Her birthday was coming up, and before any of this had happened, I'd already sent a check, as usual. A few days later it came

back in the mail with a note saying, "Thanks for the thought."
A week or so later I sent a short but to my mind loving e-mail
saying that maybe things would change in time but I just didn't
feel comfortable talking at the moment. Her response was to
e-mail back saying she was blocking me as she didn't want to
live in "fear" that I'd write again. *Don't worry,* I thought. *You're
the LAST person I'd write to now.* I could, of course, have consulted my spiritual director at any point during this time. But
why bother, when the situation was obvious: I was 100 percent
right and my sister was 100 percent wrong.

Not long afterward, though, I had coffee with my friend Father
Terry. Father Terry (who gets a whole chapter later!) lives in the
rectory at St. Basil's, is a drug and alcohol liaison for the Archdiocese of L.A., and used to have a very small problem with substance
abuse himself. He hasn't had a drink in over 30 years, and is now
a monsignor: much loved and well respected by the legions who
seek his spiritual guidance. Anyway, on this particular morning
at Starbucks, Terry described a little theory he'd worked up about
difficult people. He said when you're dealing with someone who's
difficult, you'll find that the person is generally trying to force you
into one of two positions: into either being a doormat or into
assuming an adversarial position—it's as if the person wants to
get you to teach him or her a lesson, to get you to return his or her
psychological violence with your own. And he said there's a middle
way—the way of Christ—which is to stand tall and hold the other
person accountable, but with total love: not by accusing, or pointing the finger, or laying out your case, but by refusing to pretend
that you don't "see what you see or smell what you smell."

Now I was perfectly willing to concede that while I thought

Meddy was being difficult, she thought I was being difficult, too. Whatever the case, Father Terry's paradigm seemed a very handy thing to keep in mind, especially since virtually every friend and family member I have is, like me, a spiritually wounded alcoholic/drug addict. I did get that "like me" was the operative phrase: for years I'd been examining my patterns and asking for help and trying to do better when it came to interacting with others. I was already familiar, for example, with the loving-with-detachment mantra: I didn't cause the other person's problems, couldn't cure them, couldn't control them. I was already familiar with the folly of thinking that if only the other person would change, that would make *me* happy. I was already familiar with the amazing phenomenon of taking responsibility for my part in a dispute even when there appeared to be about a 97 percent chance the other person wasn't going to look at his or hers.

I don't know if you've ever applied these concepts—I myself applied them all too seldom—but applying them at all evinced a new freedom and joy in which I found I wasn't quite so apt to try to manipulate people into doing and saying and giving me what I wanted. Changing in this way felt so good I was beginning to see it was maybe one of the things Christ was talking about when he said the kingdom of heaven is like a treasure hidden in a field, or a pearl of great price: when you find it, you sell everything you have to buy it (Matthew 13:44–45). In fact, as I said, I would have tried looking at my part here—with no guarantee that Meddy was going to look at hers—except, as I said, I *had* no part.

The reason I was thinking about treasures hidden in fields and pearls of great price at all, however, was that I'd started reading the daily liturgy for Mass and reflecting on it a bit as I went about my day. I'd learned that Advent (beginning with the first vespers of the Sunday that falls on or closest to November 30 and ending at Christmas) and Lent (roughly six weeks lasting from Ash Wednesday to Easter) are the year's two major seasons. The others, I learned, are the Christmas season (first vespers of Christmas until the Sunday after Epiphany), the Easter season (the 50 days from Easter Sunday to Pentecost), and the other 33 or 34 weeks of the year, "Ordinary Time." I'd learned there's a three-year cycle (A, B, C) for Sunday Mass, a one-year cycle of readings on the weekdays of Advent, Christmas, and Lent, and a two-year cycle (even and odd years) for the First Readings and responsorial psalm for weekdays in Ordinary Time. I'd learned there are solemnities, feast days, and memorials, that it's all sort of complicated and thrilling, and that all over the world the Church is observing and celebrating the same liturgy on the same day.

But mostly I learned that by reading a passage or two from Scripture, day after day, I started to develop a relationship with Christ. I started to feel the force of his personality and to respond. I caught something of his patience, generosity, courage, strength, sensitivity, courtliness, and strangeness, and began to be slowly enkindled with it. Instead of using my own intellect to find fault and criticize, I could use my mind to ponder this person who, no matter which way I turned him, became someone I could admire, marvel at, delight in, worship, be stimulated by, love. Instead of feeling sorry for myself, I could ponder what it must have been like for Christ to have been crucified, knowing he hadn't done one thing wrong. I could sit with Jesus for a while in the Garden of Gethsemane, where, the night before he

122 | *Heather King*

died, he was in such anguish he sweat tears of blood. I could,
and did, read G. K. Chesterton's biography of St. Francis of Assisi:
poet, romantic, embracer of "Lady Poverty," recipient, near the
end of his life, of the stigmata: the five wounds of Christ.

Some writers, Chesterton observed, have

> found things like the Stigmata a stumbling-block because
> to them religion was a philosophy. It was an impersonal
> thing; and it is only the most personal passion that provides
> here an earthly parallel. A man will not roll in the snow for
> a stream of tendency by which all things fulfill their law of
> being. He will not go without food in the name of some-
> thing, not ourselves, that makes for righteousness. He will
> do things like this, or pretty nearly like this, under quite a
> different impulse. He will do these things when he is in
> love. . . . St. Francis . . . was a Troubadour. . . . He was, to the
> last agonies of asceticism, a Troubadour. He was a lover. He
> was a lover of God and he was really and truly a lover of
> men; possibly a much rarer mystical vocation. . . .

A man will not roll in the snow except out of love, and a man—
especially if he's a prideful, stubborn, self-righteous woman—will
not let go of an argument either. One day a few months into our
feud I received a letter from Meddy. "I am so mad at you!" it said,
among other things. "How can you do this to me!" With bordering-
on-amused indifference, I read it over several times. Under different
circumstances, I might have liked to reply, but how could I agree
to disagree when she'd neglected to play fair? How could she possibly imagine I would ever speak to her again? It was progress that

I wasn't obsessively mulling over a reply, I told myself. I wouldn't *deign* to reply. I simply could not in all good conscience continue a relationship with someone whose belief system, personal dynamic, and view of life were so exponentially different than mine.

Still, my conscience had begun to niggle, and, as a last resort, I finally went to my spiritual director—not for guidance, but for corroboration. I laid out my case, omitting no detail. I emphasized my refusal, for once in my life, to be a people-pleasing chump. I leaned back and waited to bask in her approval. To my shock, she instead asked, "How often did you talk to your sister?" "I don't know," I replied. "Maybe a couple of times a week?" "How long have you had this relationship?" she asked. "I don't know," I said, "fourteen, fifteen years?" "You've had a close relationship with your sister for fifteen years and you're just going to *turn your back on her?*" she queried. "Seems to me this might be time for the St. Francis prayer."

The St. Francis prayer! Which I happened to know began, "Let me be a channel of Thy peace. . . ." Which continued, in part, "It is better to understand than to be understood, to love than to be loved. . . ." I was supposed to *continue to have a relationship with my sister?* In all that time, including while reading Chesterton's biography, the St. Francis prayer had not once entered my consciousness. I'd prayed for my sister, all right: that my airtight reasoning would bring her to the truth. That she would see the painfully sad error of her ways. That she'd repent of her sins, realize how deeply blessed she was to have me as a sibling, and beg my forgiveness. And now, it seemed, I'd mistaken being angry and hurt for having principles. I thought I'd been standing up for myself, but I'd only been being mean.

So over the next couple of weeks, and against my better judgment, I prayed the St. Francis prayer. I prayed that my sister would get all the things I wanted for myself: money, good health, love. And after a while my thinking began to change. After a while it came to me that I get to assess any given situation; I'm always allowed to have an opinion. But I'm never allowed to hate, or be patronizing, or shut the person I'm dealing with out of my heart. The minute I start thinking, *I can't in all good conscience consort with this person, this person is so pathetically misguided,* I'm sunk. We're all sinners, we're all misguided, we're all blind to our own faults and experts at ferreting out the faults of others. We're humans: we step on each other's feet sometimes, we make mistakes, we misunderstand each other. And so even though the person might have hurt my feelings unbelievably, even though I desperately want the last word, even though I'm convinced a jury would find in my favor, I set the person free. It doesn't make any more "sense" than rolling in the snow does, and we don't have to be best friends, but in that calculating little part of my brain where I like to hold grudges, I do have to let the person off the hook.

In the end, I decided Meddy and I had both been a little bit wrong and a little bit right. I apologized to my beloved sister for shutting her out (*Why do people never apologize to* me, I wondered: *wrong thought!*), and then I let it go. We don't agree on everything, but why should we? She's become my lodestar on road trips: I check in with her while I'm driving, just so someone in the world knows where I am; she tells me about her cats and songwriting, and reports on whether I have any e-mail. I appreciate her spiritual insights and wisdom, her patience and loyalty, her refusal to pander. "She's like you," she observed of a friend recently. I waited for her to fill in the blank: pretty? I thought hopefully. Humble? Smart? "She always has to be the center of attention," she concluded.

The principle is the same on a small scale or a large scale, whether the violence is psychological, or physical, or both. And since we're all connected, I have to believe that making peace on a small scale helps toward making peace on a large scale. If I want President Bush to stop the war in Iraq, I can sign a petition, send a letter to my congressperson, picket the White House. But maybe the first thing I can do is reconcile with my little sister.

CHAPTER 10

O long life! O painful life! O life that is not lived! Oh, what lonely
solitude, how incurable! What remedy do you provide for one who
finds so little on earth that might give some rest apart from you?

—St. Teresa of Ávila

For a long time I thought spiritual progress, when and if it
came, would be elevated, loud, cataclysmic. I thought my duty
was to save the entire continent of Africa, or become a swami.
As I continued to attend Mass, pray the Psalms, and read the
Gospels, however, the more I came to believe in the value of the
small, the quiet, the anonymous (although not *that* anonymous,
I guess, or I wouldn't be writing this). The more I craved to be
recognized, the more I seemed to spend many hours a day doing
things nobody knew about or could see.

I am pretty sure that if everyone did a few simple things—
observed an hour of silence, prayed for an hour, looked, really
looked, for an hour each day—the world would be transformed.
The problem is that though such a way of life sounds simple, it
is actually very hard to sustain. It requires being either indepen-
dently rich or willing to live in a certain amount of financial
precariousness ("Still Poor, still Dirty," a friend once observed
after visiting William Blake); it requires either living alone or

with someone who is, if not in solidarity, at least in sympathy with this somewhat odd bent; and it requires *wanting* to live in some sense apart from the world, having the kind of nervous system that craves solitude, quiet, routine.

Hardly anything has more solitude, quiet, and routine built into it, of course, than writing: the reflection and mental preparation that precede it, the writing itself, and, in my case, what increasingly came after: a long, solitary walk. Walking has the attributes of all the truly great gifts: it's ordinary, simple, and free. It's good exercise, probably the optimum speed at which human beings should move, and perfect for thinking and observing. Walking, I figured things out and processed things and calmed myself down, and even though I eventually explored just about every street within a three-mile radius of my apartment, I usually ended up taking one of two favorite routes each day. One was up and down the streets in Hancock Park, a wealthy neighborhood of graceful mansions and stately trees a short drive from my apartment, and the other was through the insanity of Western Avenue east to the quiet of Windsor Square and back.

Taking the same walk each day soothed me, and I came to think of the things I saw and smelled along the way as friends. I had favorite flowers: the riot of sweet peas on Norton, the passion flower twining through the chain-link fence of an abandoned lot on Eighth. I had a favorite tree: the old pepper tree near Lucerne whose branches spread the whole length of a French-windowed brick sleeping porch. I had a favorite house: my friend Judy's on Van Ness, with the English cottage garden in back, and the Japanese maple in front, and the white sweetheart roses cascading over the pergola. I had streets I loved because of the light, or the hushed quiet, and streets I avoided because of dogs, or construction, or puddles of standing water.

If St. Gregory's over on South Bronson was open, I sometimes stopped in to pray, or more often just to kneel, so happy to be in an old neighborhood Catholic church, with its scarred wooden pews, its fussy altar, its smell of furniture polish and faded flowers. I always happened upon a few other folks: an elderly Korean lady fretfully fingering a rosary (*They never come visit!*), a delicate-looking young man, head buried in his hands (*I got my girlfriend pregnant! Help!*). Sometimes I think the whole reason I converted to Catholicism is because its churches are open all day. My career in the bars was at bottom a search to belong, and I have always had a sense of almost abject gratitude for open doors, spots to rest, the opportunity to sit quietly near people without having to talk to them.

Back out in the open air walking, I learned to observe, admire, praise. I began to see that spirituality is not elevated, it's as simple as bread—so simple we don't recognize it: a leaf on the sidewalk, the shadow cast by a roof. I started to see that life is a series of small choices: the choice between moving toward yourself or toward other people, toward God. I started to see that the "spiritual" person isn't the one in the white robe: it's the one who smiles back, who lets you get through the intersection before gunning the car, who tends his or her front yard and makes the street beautiful for everyone. I started to believe that the movement away from self, no matter how small, has infinite effects.

I'm reminded of a story told by the late Bill Wilson, founder of Alcoholics Anonymous. Newly sober, and on a business trip to Akron, Ohio, Bill stood in the lobby of his hotel. He was still shaky, but the one thing he had going for him was his newfound knowledge of how one sober alcoholic could help another simply by telling his or her story. At one end of the lobby a glass case contained a directory of local churches. At the other end was a bar. Hearing the tinkle of ice and gay laughter, Bill itched to head for the bar. *Alcoholics Anonymous* describes Bill's imagined thoughts: "What about his responsibilities—his family and the men who would die because they would not know how to get well—ah yes, those other alcoholics? There must be many such in this town. He would phone a clergyman."

So instead of going to the bar, he went to the directory of churches. Instead of going to the bar, he wrote down a number. Instead of going to the bar, he went to the phone booth and lifted the receiver. And in that moment, in the lobby of a nondescript hotel in Akron, Ohio, millions and millions of lives were saved by this far-from-perfect man who desperately needed help himself and, by some divine grace, intuited it would come from helping someone else. By this man who, like many of us, would rather die alone than go to the trouble of interacting with the rest of the human race.

I have been a loner all my life. In fact, I've spent so much time alone I'm sometimes embarrassed by it; there seems something shameful about the inability or unwillingness to better adapt to human company. It's not that people don't like me (for *your* information!); or that I don't like other people; or that I'm not a good friend, which I at least marginally am. For a long time I thought there was something wrong with me that I was alone so much. Then for a long time I felt sorry for myself. Then I started to see that my loneliness is everyone's loneliness, and that I should quit trying to resist it, or fix it; I started to see that loneliness has richness and depth, and that Christ is right in the middle of it.

I recently listened to a series of lectures by Richard Rohr, the Franciscan priest and contemplative. Rohr made what struck me as a brilliant observation. He said the opposite of holding on to control isn't—as we tend to think—letting go. He said the opposite of holding on is *participating in something larger than ourselves.* I'd never thought to put it that way, but participating in something greater than myself had been exactly my experience in getting sober. Twenty years ago, my own first choice for how to get sober would have been to do so completely by myself, and my second would have been to do it with people I'd hand-picked to be as much like me as was humanly possible. So when my parents shipped me off to a Minnesota treatment center, and I found myself thrown in with the most random, arbitrary assortment of people imaginable, I just couldn't see how it was going to work. *I'm a lawyer, for God's sake,* I was thinking; *like this housewife from Iowa is going to have anything to say to me.* It wasn't so much that I was snotty as that I was afraid, but whatever the case—and whether you want to call what was at work God, or spiritual principles, or the ever-changing group as a whole—these women broke me open. They invited me into the circle, they shared their stories, their joy and pain, their jokes, and they broke me open. They were participating in something greater than themselves; they invited me to participate, too; and somehow, sometime during those 30 days, what couldn't have happened, shouldn't have happened, I had no right to have happen, did: the obsession to drink was lifted.

That was the beginning of my coming to see it's not the person who insists upon being alone who's different, but the person who's willing to admit he or she is like everyone else. Anyone can isolate himself or herself, but to cast our lot with the rest of humanity requires a kind of radical humility: a willingness to participate even though we can never tweak things or people into being the way we want them to be, and even though participating doesn't necessarily assuage the loneliness either. It's a difficult balance: not to resist the loneliness, but not to indulge in or cultivate it either. We're all so afraid of losing our uniqueness, but the world keeps us in all the loneliness we'll ever need: the world and our own temperaments make us more different, isolated, and alone than we'll ever want to be.

A lot of the time Mass isn't particularly the way I want it to be either. My fellow parishioners aren't people I'd necessarily choose for friends; someone's always brought a wailing baby, and it's easy to find fault with the architecture, priest, art, and especially music (if I were Pope, the first thing I'd do is ban most post–Vatican II hymns and all guitar Masses). Still, I invariably leave Mass feeling a little more peaceful, charitable, hopeful, and trusting than when I arrived. That is my purpose on earth: to put my body, attention, good cheer, and desire to do better, such as they are, into the stream of life, at the service of others.

The Eucharist is the ultimate participation in something greater than myself, and the fact that it *requires* participation reminds me that, much as I'd often like to, I can't trod the spiritual path alone. I'm pretty sure that when Jesus said, "I am the way, and the truth, and the life. No one comes to the Father except through me" (John 14:6), he wasn't saying that if I'm not Catholic, I'm going to hell. I think maybe he was saying that if I don't come through him, in contact with him—which is the reality of my own broken self, and my broken brothers and sisters—then I'm going to miss the gift. I think maybe he was saying that the flesh-and-blood human encounter, in all its messiness, its awkwardness, its necessary incompleteness, is the way we come to God.

Which is why, instead of attempting to save the entire continent of Africa (as if I'd be qualified, or have the energy to, and assuming Africa even wanted to be "saved"), I have become a firm, firm believer in the act that isn't going to get me anywhere and is inconvenient and involves interacting with another person. For years, I railed against the seemingly constant stream of phone calls and e-mails I seemed to get from people needing help, comfort, or to share a joke: *When am I ever going to get any work done?* I inwardly keened. Then I realized this *was* my "work" (not to mention what was making me feel needed and therefore probably keeping me alive). I find that bringing a dessert to a birthday potluck, or attending the graduation-from-kindergarten ceremony of a friend's kid, or driving some narcissistic-personality-disordered complainer who annoys the living crap out of me across town, is often just what's needed when I'm on the verge of calling 911 and begging to be carted off to the psych ward.

I don't mean just for the sake of doing something senseless, or hard, or that I don't want to do, but for the sake of doing something with a heart open enough to realize that, number one,

I'm just as bereft, clueless, and personality-disordered as the next guy or gal, and number two, that I need to allow my life to touch others', *and I need to allow theirs to touch mine.* The person I'm giving a ride to will inevitably recite a little poem, or say something weird—"I wonder what the poor people are doing," or "Old Man Time's a son-of-a-bitch," or "My wife called my mother a whore!"—and if all else fails, I'll just ask a bunch of questions and he or she will respond with something funny and human. Then, when I'm headed home gazing dully out the windshield, or swearing like a stevedore (*Why does everybody have to drive those tanks nowadays?*), or feeling sorry for myself because as usual I'm *so so ALONE*, it's not quite as bad as it usually is.

I might be a little bitter, I might be thinking, *Oh, that's pleasant, that's fair, everybody else gets to have a nice house and a nice husband and have everything go right, all the time, and constant constant love, and I get to give crazy people rides home! Through the smog-spewing, gridlocked L.A. traffic! Thank you, God!* But deep down, something's moved. I'm grateful I'm in good enough shape to be of any kind of help. I've been reminded that everyone—the people driving the tanks, the maddeningly slow-moving clerk at the post office, the poor soul of a homeless guy blocking the sidewalk with his shopping cart—wants the same thing. Everyone wants things to go smoothly, to feel useful, to be accepted; everyone is dying for a crumb of attention, of kindness.

My spiritual giant of a friend Maudie was saying one day that when we're focused on what others can give us—adulation, approval—and they don't (which is basically always), then it puts us in a constant state of "disappointment and longing." Whereas if we can focus not on what the world can give us but what we can bring to it, things are always set right. Hers is a message I can never hear enough: that everything we really long for is always right here, right now, because it is always in our power to orient our hearts toward God, toward giving instead of getting. The whole secret of life is not minding what happens—"Behold the handmaid of the Lord; let it be done to me according to Thy word"—and while we're not minding, giving. That's what creates the space in which, invisibly, imperceptibly—while we "slumber" by attending to other people's wounds—our own incurable wounds are healed.

My friend Jeff Behrens, a monk at the Monastery of the Holy Spirit in Conyers, Georgia, writes, "Jesus asks that we lay down our lives for each other in friendship, in service, in love. It is not an easy thing to do. It is easy to write about but not easy to live." He's right: in fact, it's *so* not easy that without a kind of ongoing consent to the crucifixion of my ego, it would be impossible. I'm not talking about some smarmy "Oh, I'm going to go around being *nice* to everyone" project, which, as anyone who's ever tried it knows, lasts about five minutes. I'm talking about a whole different way of seeing the world and being in the world: a consenting to be emptied.

A passage from St. Paul's letter to the Philippians runs:

. . . though he was in the form of God,
[Jesus] did not deem equality with God
as something to be exploited,
but emptied himself,
taking the form of a slave,
being born in human likeness. (Philippians 2:5–7)

That's what I'm called to—what we're all called to: a willing-ness to be emptied, to be servants. It translates into a general policy of not withholding, of being available, of offering up my whole self: not just in certain areas, not just to the people I can get something out of. It doesn't mean inviting every person I meet in the street to move in, but it does mean recognizing that I'm in a relationship with every person I meet in the street; in fact, I'm in a relationship with every person, period. I don't get to say to myself, "Oh, she is a lowly telephone receptionist who is used to people being rude," or "That is my landlord, who we both know is ripping me off: why have a charitable thought about him?" or "It's my mother, she *has* to love me no matter how crabby I am." When my heart is broken, I get to sit for a while with someone whose heart is broken, too. On the days when I feel I could die and no one would notice, I get to praise the flowers, the sun, a leaf.

So the small act matters, and we don't know where, if at all, the seed falls. After a while, we don't care where it falls. We begin to sense that nothing is wasted, no act goes unseen. "Pray to your Father who is in secret; and your Father who sees in secret will reward you," Jesus said (Matthew 6:6), and "Even the hairs of your head are all counted" (Matthew 10:30). The small act doesn't bring success, it brings peace. It may not bring riches, but it brings at least an occasional moment of acceptance. It might not change anybody or anything else—but it changes us.

CHAPTER 11

When it gets dark, one lights another candle, and when that candle is burned down, one lies quietly in the darkness. Just because there are so many mansions in my Father's house, one should make no noise.

—Franz Kafka, suffering with TB, from a letter dated March 1921

One January afternoon, less than a year after my father's death, I breezed into the lobby of Good Samaritan Hospital in downtown L.A. Glancing at the heart-shaped Mylar balloons, the saccharine greeting cards, the cheesy arrangements of carnations and baby's breath that crammed the window of the gift store, I heaved a sigh of compassion for the poor folks who were sick, thinking how depressing it would be, lying in bed surrounded by that schlock. Then I clipped a visitor's badge to my arty black sweater, took the elevator to the second floor, and signed in at the radiology department. Under "Reason for Visit," I wrote: "Mammogram."

I'd purposely taken the last available appointment of the day; the waiting room seemed eerily still. The only other patient was an old African-American woman with bandaged legs, dozing in a wheelchair. Sickly fluorescent light shone wanly from the ceiling, photos of bland desert sunsets decked the walls, and, below a sign reading COFFEE FOR PATIENTS ONLY, the hot plate sat empty.

A pleasant young gal with the Virgin of Guadalupe tattooed on her neck made a copy of my insurance card, typed some information into her computer, and told me to take a seat. Littered over chairs, strewn across end tables, and overflowing from plastic holders bolted to the counter were copies of a breast cancer magazine called *MAMM*. The name made me snicker: Tim and I had recently seen a friend in a stage production of *Little Women*, and he'd taken to calling me Marmie. Marm. Are you coming to bed, Marm? I'm going out, Marm, do we need anything at the store? A marmogram.

I picked up a copy of *MAMM*, opened it at random to a table showing survival statistics, and quickly put it down. I'd had a mammogram every year since I turned forty, seven years earlier, and though I always acted as if I were performing a civic duty under mild duress, as if the appointments were a big waste of time because of *course* I was fine, deep down they made me nervous. It seemed so unfair—if so typically one of life's little ironies—that the payoff for conscientiousness might be disfigurement, suffering, death.

I sighed, glanced at the clock, and settled into a book I'd recently checked out of the library: Rilke's *Letters to a Young Poet.* "In the deepest places of your heart," I began reading, "acknowledge to yourself whether you would have to die if it were denied to you to write."

"Miss *King!*" I heard, and glanced up to see a surly looking young woman in an Op-Art smock.

"Right here," I said, scrambling for my papers and purse.

"You were reading," she said accusingly. "I called your name twice and you just kept on *reading*."

"Sorry," I mumbled. My forays into the real world are halting and timid, and I enjoy them for only limited periods of time, like visits to relatives, until I retreat back to my books.

I followed her down the hall to a windowless room where she barked, "Undress from the waist up."

I changed behind a makeshift curtain and emerged in the cotton johnny she'd given me: a shapeless garment with a missing tie so that I had to clutch the two sides together against my torso. Against one wall, a beige metal machine hulked like an insect. I approached tentatively.

"Turn to the right," the technician said, hefted my left breast onto a glass plate, and electronically lowered a second piece of glass to within about a sixteenth of an inch of the first, leaving my flesh compressed in a painful, viselike grip. It was hard to believe one breast could cover so much ground; squished out flat down there, it looked like a pie crust.

She stepped behind a screen to take a picture, repeated the procedure on the other side, and slapped some labels on the slides. "I'm running these down to the radiologist," she threw over her shoulder. "Have a seat." Then she disappeared down the hall.

I perched on the edge of a plastic chair and opened my book, but I was too nervous to read. I tried to empty my mind, like the mystic contemplatives I so admired, but I kept willing her to hurry up: I wanted to be home by six before Tim left for the night shift at County Hospital, where he worked as a nurse in intensive care. When the tech finally cruised back in, I was all set to jump up, get dressed, and bolt. And then she uttered the ten words that changed my world.

"The doctor wants a second picture of your left breast," she announced, casually loading a new slide.

Adrenaline jolted through my body like electricity, my brain pulsing: CANCER! CANCER!! CANCER!!!

"*Why?*" I pleaded, in a weirdly loud voice.

"Oh, he thinks he might have seen a little shadow," she said, impatiently waving me back to the machine.

I paused for a moment, then shuffled over, weak with fright.

"Relax," she commanded; rarely at ease under the best of circumstances, my body now had all the pliability of a rigor mortis victim. She lowered the glass plate again—"DON'T MOVE!"—ran behind the screen to take some more pictures, and, for the second time, disappeared down the hall.

I slunk back to the chair and waited, my breath shallow, the way it is when you wake from one of those nightmares where the monster, having steadily gained ground, is panting down your neck. After a while I realized my heart was beating in rhythm to *Hail Mary, full of grace, the Lord is with thee. . . .* I looked down at my arms. They were purple with cold and I'd never noticed before how thin my wrists were. *Blessed art thou among women and blessed is the fruit of thy womb, Jesus. . . .*

I had never paid much attention to my body, which is perhaps why it was the one area of my life that was characterized by moderation and common sense, that radiated health, that wasn't fraught with anxiety and neurosis. I hadn't had a drink in twelve years or a cigarette in ten, I exercised, I ate grains and fruits and stout dark greens like broccoli and rapini, and that was about it for my personal-care regimen. I had no truck with vitamin nuts or people who ate only organic food; I considered nutritionists, chiropractors, and acupuncturists to be a bunch of overpaid quacks; and as if to underscore my point, I hadn't had so much as a cold or the flu in years.

Partly this stemmed from the fact that I was way too impatient to devote special care to a body that was already sturdy and serviceable, and partly I'd inherited this attitude from my dyed-in-the-wool Yankee mother, who classifies ginger ale as a medicine, considers Novocain a snobbish extravagance, and, after the birth of her last child, had gone 29 years without seeing a doctor. I'd always considered Mom slightly over-the-top on the subject, but I had to admit that I, too, had come to treat my body firmly and without emotion, the way you would a dependable tractor.

Take a walk, I'd snort to myself when people with modern, vaguely defined conditions like chronic fatigue syndrome or fibromyalgia started complaining. In New Hampshire, where I grew up, people didn't go to doctors: they worked. They laid brick or dug vegetable gardens or shoveled snow, and, though I had always shrunk from those particular activities as way too strenuous and difficult myself, I still saw exercise as the surest way of staying healthy, and I couldn't stomach the rarefied idea of paying money to do it. I walked to the library or bank or grocery store, I took ten-mile hikes in the mountains, I played two-hour, hard-pitched singles tennis matches. On summer afternoons, I drove up to the battered courts at L.A. Community College, where tufts of grass grew between the cracked green clay, and hit old balls against the wall for practice. As I worked on my backhand in the blazing sun, it was a little point of pride that I still weighed about the same as when I'd played basketball in high school.

Still, lately I'd started to feel protective and slightly sad about my aging body: the blue-green varicose vein that had sprung up on my left calf, the loose skin on my upper arms that quivered when I caught myself off guard in the mirror. And now, quaking in the corner of the mammogram room, I thought frantically, *I'm not old enough to get breast cancer!* Chronologically, I was middle-aged, but, with my nervous system—no, I was not a good candidate for any illness, especially not a plague universally loathed and feared, one of the most horrifying words in the English language: "cancer." Half an hour earlier I'd imagined myself to be in the prime of life. Now I saw myself hairless, shrunken, still wearing this same ill-fitting johnny with the missing tie. . . .

The technician flounced back in, snapped her gum, and said, "Okay, you can get dressed."

I rose from my seat, trembling. "So . . . did he say anything?" I asked. "Is it . . ."

"Wanna put your address on here?" she said, pushing a white envelope across the table. "You'll get the results in two weeks."

Before I could ask anything else, she was in the back room dialing her cell phone. "Yeah, so eight fifty for the roof and what about the window frames?" she was saying as I left. I gave her a little wave, but she never looked up.

That was the beginning of my thankfully short, and, to date, only, bout with Western medicine, an enterprise which, paradoxically in light of its billing as a "helping profession," seemed to run on a deep desire to have as little actual human interaction as possible. There was the inept office staff who, when the mammogram results came back with a big black X beside ABNORMAL, kept "losing" my authorization request for a biopsy. "Oh no," Dolores would say sadly, "we haven't gotten to that at *all*. Myrna's sitting all alone in the back room by the computer with just a big *stack* of those things." There was the oncological surgeon who stuck a giant needle in my breast, sucked out a hunk of tissue, and left a big pan of what looked like bloody chicken fat about two feet away from the examining table, right where I could see it. There was my "personal care" physician, who gave me the results— invasive ductal carcinoma—over the phone, at five o'clock on a Friday night.

"You mean . . . ?" I faltered.

"Malignant," he confirmed. "Put in a request Monday for a surgeon," and he signed off, leaving me to contemplate what— until I snapped into action the next week, got a copy of the pathology report, and began conducting my own research—I took to be my imminent death. People sometimes do die shortly after being diagnosed with breast cancer, and it seemed needlessly cursory and cruel to deliver such news and then withhold even the most basic information about what it might mean.

I'd never realized it before, but I'd always assumed that God had given me good (and invincible, and perpetual) physical health as compensation for my congenitally fragile emotional health. I'd seriously thought I was immune to illness, and it came as a shock not only to discover my physical vulnerability but that God and I weren't quite on the footing I'd thought. I hadn't quite grasped the harsh beauty of the fact that God's ways are not our ways; that the rain falls on the just and the unjust (not that I was so just, but everybody tends to think they're just and "the others" aren't); that justice doesn't consist in the meting out of suffering in equal measure but in the fact that, to the precise degree that we trust in God's love—to that degree, and more—we will be open to feel and receive it.

Maybe that's why the person who sticks in my mind from that time wasn't a member of the oh-so-impersonal medical profession: it was a fellow sufferer. Back then, I had one over-riding emotion: self-centered, panic-stricken fear. I didn't know that eventually I'd be fine, that the lumpectomy scar would be barely visible, that weeks would go by where the word "cancer" never entered my thoughts. Back then, the diagnosis still fresh, I thought about my condition every waking and sleeping moment. So even before I had surgery, I called UCLA's Revlon Breast Center and signed up for their second-opinion clinic.

The building, 200 Medical Plaza, was on upper Westwood Blvd., a huge state-of-the-art building, reeking of power and money, designed to telegraph the message that I was going to have some A-1 solid citizens behind me when I stepped through its plateglass doors. With its "Plastic Surgery Suite," "Reflections Boutique," and six-foot-high floral arrangements, the place said loud and clear: *This is serious, but we're in control, calling the shots, and resolutely antideath.* Two floors down, the Revlon Center featured thick noise-muffling carpet, teak paneling, and a staff that had obviously been carefully trained to be pleasant, supportive, and cheery. A receptionist smiled blandly, took my check (surprise—the authorization hadn't come through in time, but I'd be reimbursed), and handed me a clipboard of forms.

I found a seat and looked around, casting clandestine glances at the other women. There were fifteen or so, ranging in age from maybe twenty-five to seventy, perched stiffly on the edges of their chairs. *They know what it's like to lie awake all night staring at the ceiling,* I thought; *they could die, too.*

"What a bunch of crap," a voice muttered, and I turned to my right to see a petite blonde, about my age, in a Dolce & Gabbana jacket and black leather pants. A cloud of Calvin Klein's "Eternity" wafted above her head. She was bent over her own stack of forms, filling in the blanks with one manicured hand and brandishing a half-eaten Whopper with the other.

"This your first time?" she asked, catching my eye and wiping a smear of mayo from the corner of her mouth.

"My *first* time? Well . . . yeah."

"First time's the worst," she reported, as if I could look forward to several more such visits. "It's my third."

"Your . . . third?" That was when I took a good look at her hair—bangs and a shoulder-length flip—and saw it was way too shiny to be real: she was wearing an ash-blond wig.

"Yeah, I'm on chemo again all right," she laughed, following my eyes. "I'll be puking my guts out by the end of the week."

"Again?" I echoed faintly.

"Oh, chemo's nothing compared to all I've been through in the last ten years," she said airily. "Double mastectomy, nerve damage in my arm, reconstructive surgery, the whole bit. Thought I was home free after the bone marrow transplant"—she paused to scrape the pickles off her hamburger—"but now it's metastasized to my liver."

Except for the wig, she looked normal, if a little ethereal: translucent skin, a blue vein tendrilling across her temple.

"I'm just buying time now," she continued. "What keeps me going, I have three teenagers at home in Newport Beach, plus my friends, and shopping. Money means zipola to me, which isn't exactly great for the old marriage"—she jerked a thumb to her left, where a long-suffering businessman type sat shuffling through some papers on top of his briefcase—"but at this point I could give two shits. The only reason I'm here is to see if they have any drugs that might give me an extra month or two."

I couldn't get my mind around it: this junk-food-eating middle-aged mall rat nonchalantly telling me that she was going to die.

"You'll be fine, though," she added, giving my knee a friendly slap. "The fear of the unknown is the worst. Actually going through it is no big deal."

All afternoon I waited in a white room while doctors filed in with their stethoscopes and file folders, their cool, probing hands. I prayed my breast wouldn't have to be maimed, I prayed they wouldn't tell me I had some mutant strain that was reproducing at an outlandishishly unheard-of rate, I prayed if I had to die of cancer, it wouldn't be for a long, long time and they'd give me lots of drugs first. At around five, the "team" came in to report their findings.

"For Stage One patients with a tumor under two centimeters and no lymph node involvement," the surgical oncologist summed it up, "the risk of recurrence is about nine percent. We'll know more after your surgery, but, for now, we think you're doing exactly the right thing."

Nine percent ran through my mind like a mantra as I got dressed and gathered up my things. *If only it's not in my lymph nodes, 9 percent's not bad. It could be a lot worse than 9 percent.* Outside the elevator, I ran into the woman with the ash-blond wig.

"How did you do?" she cried. "Good news?"

"Not bad, I guess," I admitted.

"Oh hon, that's great!" she said, leaning over to give me a big hug. "I told you you'd do fine!"

How can you describe such goodness, such bravery?—this woman who had been through hell, who was dying, saying "Good news?" as she stepped onto the elevator and the doors closed behind her, this woman who hoped someone *else* would make it.

I think of her often, this woman from Newport Beach who wore a big diamond, whose hobby was shopping, who could have treated her husband a little better. And each time I remember how, when Christ walked among his disciples after the Resurrection, nobody had recognized him.

CHAPTER 12

The century of health, hygiene and contraceptives, miracle drugs and synthetic foods, is also the century of the concentration camp and the police state, Hiroshima and the murder story. Nobody thinks about death, about his own death, as Rilke asked us to do, because nobody leads a personal life. Collective slaughter is the fruit of a collectivized way of life.

—Octavio Paz, from "The Day of the Dead" in *The Day of Solitude*

Once the news of my diagnosis really sank in, suddenly I lived in a world of cancer: every magazine article about cancer, every obituary of someone who had died of cancer. Convinced my own was spreading by the second, every two minutes I felt a pain in my head (brain tumor), ribs (lung tumor), or side (ovary tumor). I immediately went out to the local Borders and bought the bible of breast cancer, *Dr. Susan Love's Breast Book*, but it was far from comforting. "If one cell has left the breast and is sitting alone, somewhere else in your body, untouched by the immune system," one passage read, "the most extensive mastectomy in the world won't keep the cancer from returning. *That cell will multiply and the cancer will grow*" (emphasis mine). One thing I knew going into surgery: I wanted every treatment they had. I was going to demand radiation. I was going to beg for hormone drugs. I was going to make them give me about a year of the strongest chemo they had.

"My" and "lumpectomy" were two words I'd hoped never to use consecutively, but the event came to pass nonetheless. A week or so later, I drove to Good Samaritan once again, this time to meet with an oncologist to discuss the findings. My lymph nodes were clear—a huge relief, as it meant the cancer hadn't started spreading. Because the lymph nodes weren't involved and my tumor was under two centimeters, the dividing line between Stage 1 and 2, I was a Stage 1. Cancer is also assigned a grade based on the aggressiveness of the tumor: the lowest possible grade was 1A; mine was 1B. I was estrogen and progesterone positive, which was good partly because hormone-positive tumors grow slightly more slowly than hormone-negative tumors, and also because it meant I'd be responsive to tamoxifen. In light of these findings, a breast cancer "team" had met that morning to discuss my treatment plan, the oncologist told me, and they'd been split. Half had recommended four months of adriamycin and cytoxan (there were two basic types of chemo administered to breast cancer patients—a "low-test" called CMF, and a "high-test"; this was the high-test), radiation, and a five-year course of tamoxifen; the other half had recommended radiation and tamoxifen only.

Naturally, he had neither the time nor inclination to even rudimentarily explain any of this, so when it came to the about two million questions that rose to mind the minute I left his office, I knew I was on my own. Chemo was by far the most severe and invasive of the treatments, so I thought I'd start there and do a little online research. Chemo was horrible, but it would make me better—wouldn't it? Chemo was the worst, but I'd do it so I'd live—right? Plowing through the daunting number of breast cancer sites was a feat in itself, and poring over the inevitable multiple sets of cross-referencing statistics was like grappling with a spreadsheet. I'd finally find a halfway useful article and it would say something like "Combined with radiation, for Stage 2, node-positive, post-menopausal women with tumors over 2 cm, one 1988 study showed that chemotherapy reduces the risk of recurrence by 28.5%." That was fine, but what of my situation: Stage 1, node-negative, premenopausal, and with a tumor *under* not only two, but under one centimeter? What had post-1988 research shown? What were the survival, as opposed to the recurrence, rates?

Still, it didn't take a research expert to figure out that chemo was one gnarly treatment. A systemic therapy that treated the whole body by interfering with the process of cell division, it was administered intravenously, and, because it worked on all rapidly dividing cells, it unfortunately killed not only cancer cells but hair cells, intestinal wall cells, and bone marrow cells as well. Consequently, head hair fell out; eyebrows, eyelashes, pubic hair, leg and arm hair fell out; and, in many cases, fingernails and toenails fell off. Adriamycin could leak out of the veins and cause burns so severe they required skin grafting.

Chemo could cause nausea and vomiting, hot flashes and induced menopause. *People died from chemo.* According to Dr. Ralph Moss, author of *The Cancer Industry,* "Chemotherapy often brings in its train a host of blood-deficiency diseases. . . . These, in turn, can give rise to massive, uncontrollable infections. Cancer patients on chemotherapy have been known to die of something as innocuous as the common cold." But what really floored me was that chemo didn't even do that much good, especially—though they relentlessly pushed it anyway—for early Stage 1 patients like me. It reduced the risk of recurrence by about a third, which meant my chances of recurrence would diminish from 9 percent to 6. And even when it "worked," that usually meant two or three extra years, not the rest of a person's "natural" life. I couldn't believe that a mere few weeks earlier, I'd been mentally clamoring for this odious stuff.

I'd been thinking of radiation as a walk in the park compared to chemotherapy, almost fun. But when I consulted *Dr. Susan Love's Breast Book*, I found that, far from being a breezy little lark, radiation had side effects which included asymptomatic rib fractures; a "sunburn" effect; tiredness ("The body seems to be using all its resources to cope with the radiation, and doesn't leave much energy for anything else"); lung damage ("Depending on how your chest is built, a little of the radiation may get to your lung and give you a cough"); thickened, darker-colored skin; crusty nipples (?!); swelling and sensitivity; depression; compounding of the scarring from surgery; increased risk of lymphedema; problems with the nerves that go from the arm to the hand, causing numbness to the fingertips; costochondritis, a kind of arthritis that causes inflammation of the space between the breasts where the rib and breastbone connect ("The pain can be scary—you wonder if your cancer has spread"); and a permanent change in the feel of the breast ("It will never feel completely normal again: you'll continue to have some sharp, shooting pains from time to time—how often varies greatly from woman to woman"). Since radiation makes cells mutate, and mutated cells are what cause cancer in the first place, secondary cancers could occur. Some studies seemed to show that radiation could cause heart disease in women with cancer of the left breast. Finally, I learned one major fact my doctors had neglected to mention: because radiation above a certain dosage damages normal tissue, a breast could tolerate only a single round of it; if a second lump appeared, the only option (in the medical establishment's eyes) would be a mastectomy.

But the truly remarkable thing, the thing I had to dig deep to discover, was that though radiation might slightly reduce the risk of recurrence, *it had no discernible effect on mortality rates.**

Somehow radiation didn't sound quite so innocuous after that. Although it had been shown to reduce by 20 to 30 percent the chance of recurrence in the breast (as with chemo), if my chance was only 9 percent to begin with, was it worth risking all those side effects to reduce it to 6 or 7 percent? Also, I started thinking about that *MAMM* article I'd read in the waiting room that had pointed out that some doctors believe that the radiation

---

* See, e.g., *Breast Cancer: What You Should Know (But May Not Be Told) About Prevention, Diagnosis and Treatment,* by Steve Austin and Cathy Hitchcock: "Radiation does not improve your chances of surviving breast cancer," p. 49; *The Cancer Industry,* by Ralph W. Moss: "In a 1968 study of 3,000 women [being treated for breast cancer] at over 40 institutions, [Dr. Bernard Fisher of the University of Pittsburgh] found that those receiving postoperative radiation did no better than those receiving only surgery in the treatment of breast cancer," p. 62; and an Associated Press article titled "Drop in Breast Cancer Deaths Tied to Treatment" (*Los Angeles Times,* May 19, 2000): "Radiation, the oldest [breast cancer] treatment, prevents about two-thirds of recurrences but has yielded only a 1% decrease in the overall death rates. Although it works well in clearing up rogue bits of cancer in the breast, it also increases the risk of heart attacks and strokes."

from mammograms can cause breast cancer as well as detect it. Weren't the people who invented radiation essentially the same folks who brought us Nagasaki? Did I really want to microwave my breast?

Last, I researched tamoxifen, a hormonal therapy: in a nutshell, too much estrogen contributed to breast cancer; tamoxifen blocked estrogen and thereby supposedly prevented the growth of new tumors. The whole area of hormones vis-à-vis breast cancer, it turned out, was very confusing. "It used to be felt that women with breast cancer could never take hormones because it would be 'like pouring gasoline on a fire' and would immediately cause the cancer to flare up . . . ," Dr. Love wrote. However, "Recently the trend of putting all women on postmenopausal hormones has led us to reevaluate this premise. Physicians are noting that there are no data and have done a 180-degree switch. We used to say, 'No data so don't take it.' Now we are saying, 'No data so it's okay.'"

In fact, the way tamoxifen worked was itself a mystery. "Tamoxifen is a very peculiar drug. In some ways it blocks estrogen, as it does in the breast, but in other organs like the liver, bones and uterus, it acts like estrogen," Dr. Love explained. In the opinion of Jacob Epstein, a cancer expert/establishment gadfly, that made tamoxifen "an extremely dangerous drug . . . one of the most potent known liver carcinogens, making it likely that a significant number of healthy women receiving tamoxifen will die from liver cancer within a decade or so, without any warning of this very grave risk."

As for effectiveness, according to Epstein there was no hard evidence that tamoxifen reduced the rates of breast cancer at all, and even the conservative Dr. Love admitted, "At this point it is still not clear that, in premenopausal women, [tamoxifen] adds anything to chemotherapy or works as well as an adjuvant treatment." In fact, some research showed that though tamoxifen initially blocks estrogen in the body, thereby causing breast cancer tumors to shrink, whatever cancer cells remain eventually learn to *thrive* on the drug, with many women developing a more aggressive form of cancer later on.

Reading the newspaper each morning, I began to reflect that it was almost as if fighting evil with more evil—whether it was in my own body or the body of the world—only resulted in the original evil manifesting in another form. We kept executing criminals, and manufacturing nuclear weapons, and imposing sanctions in Iraq that had been responsible for the deaths of hundreds of thousands of children. And growing beneath, like malignant tumors, were skyrocketing suicide rates, schoolyard massacres, acts of terrorism: worse, more grotesque forms of violence than ever before.

As if on cue, I was bombarded with yet more info about the sleazier aspects of the medical community. I read that the prestigious *New England Journal of Medicine* had been exposed in several blatant conflict-of-interest situations with pharmaceutical companies. I heard on a public radio slot that, contrary to the study results—all of which, it transpired, had been completely falsified—the painful, expensive bone marrow transplants doctors had been performing on metastatic breast cancer patients did not improve survival rates at all. I called a breast cancer advocacy center in Berkeley and spoke to a woman who said that statistics have their place, but they really couldn't tell me anything about my particular disease. Breast cancer was a complex illness with innumerable factors, some of which weren't even known, she said, and therefore *everyone's case was completely different.*

If everyone was completely different, I wondered as I hung up, why did they tell everyone to have almost the exact same treatment? In fact, I was beginning to realize, "they" simply didn't know. They didn't know what caused breast cancer, they didn't know what course it would run, they didn't know what cured it. And instead of humbly admitting as much, they'd developed all kinds of harmful, noxious, invasive treatments that might or might not work, and even when they did work, they didn't work very often, and often they had side effects that were worse than the original disease.

Weary of research, I turned for a while to the (thankfully voluminous) world of sickness literature. I read *In the Country of Illness*, a book by a man named Robert Lipsyte. Robert had recovered nicely from his bout with testicular cancer, but his wife had died of breast cancer that had metastasized to her bones, all described in great detail, including the spontaneously broken ribs, the wheelchair, the black gunk running from her nose and mouth at the end. I read *In the Land of Pain*, a memoir by the nineteenth-century French writer Alphonse Daudet about his excruciating run with syphilis. I read Susan Sontag's *Illness as Metaphor*, the gist of which seemed to be: Oh, it is difficult to exist in a world where everyone but me is so deeply stupid.

It was a comfort to know I wasn't alone (obviously, in fact, I was far luckier than most women with breast cancer), and I started to realize I couldn't be alone in my concerns about treatment either. At the downtown public library, I found a whole section devoted to alternative therapies. I read books about homeopathic healing, allopathic healing, self-healing, healing through diet, all of which mentioned the apparent connection between a high incidence of breast cancer and a high-fat diet. I'd sized up my diet as relatively low fat already, but on my next trip to Trader Joe's I started reading those little fat-content labels and I couldn't believe how much fat was in, say, one tiny serving of cheese. Eggs, olives, and nuts unfortunately were also loaded with fat. Wasn't I supposed to have *some* fat, I started wondering. Wouldn't I die otherwise—of grief, if nothing else?

Over the course of the next few weeks I read *A Cancer Battle Plan* and *The Breast Cancer Prevention Diet.* I read the "cleansing diet schedule" from a place called Health Quarters Lodge. I read about the healing power of juice fasting, the effect of sugar intake on phagocytosis, the importance of an acid/alkaline balance. I read about toxic diet, toxic dentistry, and toxic emotions.

After I had read enough books and talked to enough people, I was confused. One book said to drink flaxseed oil and another said to eat only the meal. One book said to eat nothing but brown rice and seaweed, another said to eat nothing but fruits and vegetables, and one man, a friend of a friend who worked as a TV set designer and had cured himself of supposedly fatal lung cancer, told me that under no circumstances should I eat any fruit at all, because sugar feeds cancer.

Alternative diets could be darned expensive, like the Swiss

clinics where they irrigated the colon every five minutes, or a fat-fighting black walnut fungus that cost $85 an ounce. Many also seemed unnecessarily rigid: a glass of carrot juice at ten, a dish of grated beets at two, and any deviation could be fatal. That's when I decided I was not going to get too worked up about diet. Cutting down on fat had to help, but I knew if I got too fanatic about it, every "slip" would stress me out so badly I might as well start scarfing Valrhona truffles and crème fraîche three times a day.

Even the most perfect diet couldn't necessarily save my life. Some of the studies, in fact, had come to the conclusion that it wasn't so much less fat as fewer calories in general that led to a lower incidence of breast cancer. Here at last was a theory reflecting my own dawning belief that physical and spiritual healing go hand-in-hand, are in a sense the same thing. Eating less was simple, it was free, it would require a change in my whole stance toward food. It only made sense that optimum health would come from not taking more than my share, by eating with attention and love. What seemed way more important than following the letter of any particular diet was learning to treat food as part of the sacrament of life.

I cut down on sugar and coffee, I switched from cow's milk to soy, I began fasting once a week. But maybe the most radical change in my eating habits was this: when Tim and I sat down to dinner each night, I started saying grace.

That pretty much emblemized my stance toward my cancer. In the end, I went against my doctors' recommendations and

declined radiation, chemo, *and* tamoxifen. Was that a subli-
mated death wish? I don't know. Was that unhealthy? I don't
know. Who's to say in any given situation what's "healthy"? Is
it any "sicker" to go against medical advice than to, say, have a
face lift? Is it "healthier" to submit to an aggressive treatment
that may or may not work, or to refrain from it?

What would Jesus do? I kept asking myself. Would Jesus
have gotten chemo? Would Jesus have undergone radiation? I
don't know. What I do know is that illness forces us inward, and
if we get really quiet, it's almost as if our cells tell us what's
"right" for us in any given situation. And when I got really quiet
myself, I just couldn't, given my specific condition and under
the circumstances, get behind spending one minute more than
was absolutely necessary in the hands of a health-care system
that had exhibited such extraordinary coldness toward and distance from my body and soul.

I'm grateful for and awed by the wonders of modern medicine, but I distrust the pharmaceutical companies that try to
goad me into "fighting a battle," the insurance juggernauts that
tell me there's safety in expensive premiums, a culture that tells
me everything can be bought: health, happiness, time. If I'm
going to fight a battle, let it be against cynicism and hypocrisy,
against logic over mystery, against a world that tells me I'm a
fool to believe in one baptism for the forgiveness of sins, the
Communion of Saints, the Resurrection of the Body and life everlasting. In my longing for security, let it be the security of prayer.
If my cancer comes back, my goal is to move to the desert and
lie in a hammock with Gerard Manley Hopkins and Dostoyevsky

and the Psalms as my companions, and have someone bring me the Eucharist every day and, gazing out over the mountains— "Lord, I have loved the beauty of Thy house"—die in peace. Then again, it could be I'd avail myself of every "weapon" modern medicine has to offer.

But as it turns out, I may not have to do either. The medical world considers five years without recurrence a "cure." Last February marked eight for me—and I'm fine.

CHAPTER 13

When I moved to the East Side, I went to a Salesian priest, Father
Zossima. It was he who urged me to go to daily communion. I had
thought this was only for the old or the saintly, and I told him so.
"Not at all," he said. "You go because you need food to nourish you,
for your pilgrimage on this earth."

—Dorothy Day, *Loaves and Fishes*

L.A. can appear to the outsider to be a 465-square-mile
emperor with no clothes. For a long time after I moved here,
I couldn't believe that rich people drove the same featureless
freeways I did; that movie stars reached the zenith of their
careers in the Dorothy Chandler Pavilion (this was before they
moved the Academy Awards to the Kodak Theater), with its
pedestrian lobby and Liberace-style chandeliers; that immi-
grants left their unspoiled homelands only to come here and
spend their days among cheesy minimalls and prefab "food
courts." There were some pockets of town so packed with
Rite-Aids and Chevron stations, so choked with concrete and
cars, so devoid of greenery, humanity, or charm that a near-
suicidal depression engulfed me each time I passed through:
Alvarado just before it hits Glendale Boulevard, the intersection of Venice and Overland in Palms, the entire cities (that's

not really fair, but the parts of them I saw driving) of Industry, Commerce, Vernon.

Then, slowly, small treasures began to reveal themselves in the homely landscape of my day-to-day life, the way glints of gold sometimes reveal themselves to a prospector who stares long enough at a slag heap. Lilies of the Nile rose phoenixlike from litter-strewn median strips. The scent of jasmine wafted in on the evening breeze along with the thudding beat of boom boxes. From exhaust-shrouded curbs rose men selling garnet cherries, roses the color of old ivory, dusty bags of peanuts.

Over the years, deeper, richer treasures surfaced. Amid a cacophony of gunfire, circling helicopters, and ambulance sirens wailing the news that yet another Seoul-trained driver had merrily run a red light, I learned—was forced to learn—to pray. Assaulted by billboards for Disneyland, Universal Studios, and Magic Mountain, I discovered instead Huntington Gardens, the L.A. County Museum of Art, the architectural and intellectual wonders of the downtown library. If the traffic was fiendish, I eventually found that KUSC's classical music eased the pain of gridlock; if the city was crowded, all those people created an infectious level of creative energy; if it was noisy, I was that much more grateful for every moment of silence.

Partly, this was the willed optimism of a born pessimist. But the longer I lived in L.A., the more I saw that it wasn't so much that the good "balanced out" the bad—in fact, the bad, the irritating, the ugly, seemed clearly to have the upper hand—it was that the good was of a different order altogether. The guy in line ahead of me at Ralphs who noticed I had only three items and waved me through canceled out not just the cell-phone-yakking driver who'd just barreled into the parking space I'd been waiting for but the supercilious clerk at Rocket Video, the jackass who cut in line at Starbucks, and the crabby Wells Fargo teller, too. My downstairs neighbor threw his thousandth unjustified snit, but when he padded upstairs with a single bowl of minestrone soup that night, the slate was wiped clean once again. A childhood friend OD'd and died, but a new friend brought me a copy of Jane Kenyon's "Let Evening Come," and I pondered the mystery of how the smallest human touch brings comfort in the midst of the most staggering tragedy or grief. I started to feel the transformative power in this underground network of seemingly inconsequential acts, to discern a pattern. I started going to Mass and saw that scattered throughout the city, in the midst of clamor and chaos, were sanctuaries of quiet: oases of dark tranquility smelling of incense and wax. Through shoot-outs and stabbings, mudslides and earthquakes, jittery nights and adrenaline-charged days—all over the city candles burned in red glass above the Body of Christ, the deepest, most hidden mystery of all.

Going to Mass did not make me "better": my first thought, still, was usually the fearful one, the cynical one, the critical one. But I went anyway. I went because in the dimmest reaches of my confused, angst-ridden mind there was still something in me that wanted to get down on my knees and, in spite of my own shortcomings and the shortcomings of everyone around me, give thanks. I went because I was beginning to understand the parable of the yeast—that the reign of God is like yeast which a woman kneaded into three measures of flour, and eventually the whole mass of dough began to rise (Matthew 13:33).

I went because I was beginning to believe that heaven is not some other world, but shot all through the broken world where we already live.

After a while I noticed another woman at morning Mass. She had high cheekbones and short curly hair, she wore a heavy sweater and a pair of faded blue Keds, and she was white, a relative rarity in Koreatown. She didn't look rich, but she didn't look dirt poor, either. I tried to peg her: a struggling artist, a social worker, a nurse? When we greeted each other at the Sign of Peace, her hand felt like sandpaper. A sculptor? A painter? One morning I introduced myself—her name was Barbara—and, after we'd chatted a bit, I asked her what she did.

"I dance," she replied.

"A dancer!" I exclaimed, thinking Suzanne Farrell, Martha Graham, Gelsey Kirkland. "Jazz or ballet or . . . ?"

"I have to go to my lesson now," she said. "But come to Mass at St. Thomas Sunday. We'll go out for coffee after and I'll tell you all about it."

St. Thomas the Apostle is on the edge of Pico-Union, an Hispanic neighborhood so dicey that when I once passed another Anglo on the street we exchanged sickly smiles of relief, as if to say, "Nobody's shot *me* yet either. . . ." The fact that Barbara attended church and possibly even lived there intrigued me more than ever.

When I showed up Sunday, I spotted her in a pew down in front, all dolled up in a kick-pleat skirt and spectator pumps, radiating class and good cheer. The muscled calves, usually hidden beneath her jeans, rippled as she walked, and with her erect carriage and neatly turned head, she looked every bit the dancer.

Afterward we walked to her favorite pastry shop, its shelves so jam-packed with chocolate-dipped churros, pasteles de tres leche, and miniature tins of flan that the very air tasted of sugar. Barbara introduced me to the owner, the owner's sister, and the owner's granddaughter before settling us in at a table near the door.

"Hey, Maverick, where ya staying?" she called out as a crew-cut woman wearing grease-stained fatigues and a tangle of dog tags walked by.

"Still on the street," Maverick mumbled, and Barbara got up to slip her a handful of change.

By now I was dying to hear her story. "So how'd you end up in Pico-Union?" I asked. "Where do you dance? What else do you do?"

Between sips of weak coffee and bites of stale bolillo, she filled me in. She'd been raised in a Jewish household in New York City and converted to Catholicism in 1981. Then God had taken her "out of the world" for seven years, during which she lived in an ex-seminary in Italy, cooking for the priests and teaching dance.

"It was totally medieval," she reported cheerfully. "Stone walls four feet thick, cold, damp. When you opened a door bats flew out."

Now she lived in a nearby apartment; looked after six dogs, eleven cats, and her senile Armenian landlady; and rode the bus five days a week to Studio City—an hour and a half each way—for ballet classes.

"I've had the same teacher off and on for twenty-five years. He's always on my case," she laughed. " 'Some people think they don't have to work!' he says. 'Some people think they can just light a couple of candles in church.' "

Twenty-five years! Of *lessons?* Her intelligent eyes were lined with black, her head cocked like a bird. "So do you dance . . . professionally?" I asked. "I mean do you put on shows or what?"

"Not really," Barbara replied. "I don't dance for success or money or to be noticed: I do it as a form of prayer. I think of it as offering up my time and body and pain to someone who needs it more than I do. I say the rosary, one Hail Mary for each plié."

"You . . . pray?" I faltered. "You say a Hail Mary for every . . . ?"

"On weekends I shoo away the animals and set up a barre in my room," she continued, and I remembered her calluses. "When I'm really tired or discouraged, I try to think of Christ on the cross."

I fell silent for a moment, attempting to digest this scenario, to even remotely envision such a life.

"What do you do for money?" I asked finally.

"Oh, I don't need much," she said with a vague wave of her hand. "God provides. It hasn't been easy: for a long time I felt so isolated I thought I was going crazy. But eventually I learned to integrate my dancing with the rest of the world, and now my life is so rich, so incredibly abundant I can't begin to describe it. . . ."

I studied her closely, the smile brilliant but for a missing tooth at one end of the lower jaw, the turquoise angora sweater lightly matted with dog hair. *Was she a nutcase or some kind of saint?* I wondered. *Was I, with my limited vision, capable of judging? Is sainthood perfection, or is surrendering our imperfections to be transformed into something that remains invisible to most of the rest of the world?*

Barbara pointed across the street, to a man collecting bottles in a shopping cart. "I respect those people," she said. "Do you know what hard work that is? I always save my glass for them."

Then she leaned in and put a roughened hand on mine. "Hard times are coming," she whispered, "and, all over, God is planting seeds, preparing people. Not showy people, but little people. You don't know. It could be that crazy old lady begging for change on the corner who's going to save us all."

Walking down the sidewalk toward home, the brown faces shuttered against my white one, I was thinking: *How many people like Barbara can there be in the world? What are the chances of meeting one of them?* A lone man browsed a sparsely stocked record shop, candles burned from the dim interior of a botanica, and, inside a pocket-size restaurant, upside-down water glasses glinted from white tablecloths: a world parallel to mine, yet alien. The smells of spit-roasted chicken, soapy perfume, overripe bananas drifted into the street. A group of teenage girls pushed by, their tattooed young bodies clad in Lycra, their eyes saying, *Get outta my way.*

Half a block down, on the sidewalk in front of Doti's Bridal, stood a mannequin in a swirling white satin gown. Sequins sparkled like diamonds in two long rows that ran past her breasts, her flared hips, her long legs. The hem of her billowing skirt grazed two white high heels, her eyes were raised heavenward, and one hand was lifted, as if in song.

As I approached, she was like love incarnate, a transfiguration sandwiched between a nail salon and a video store: I was close enough now to touch her. That was when I saw the garland of wax flowers askew on the brittle blond hair, the missing clump of fake eyelashes, the expanse of flesh-colored plaster chest above the sweetheart neckline, veiled with a layer of gray grit.

And somehow that made her more beautiful still. Because isn't that always the way it is? And isn't it always, in the end, somehow all right?

CHAPTER 14

So be very careful how you spend your time. There is nothing more precious. In the twinkling of an eye heaven may be won or lost. God shows that time is precious, for he never gives two moments of time side by side, but always in succession.

—*The Cloud of Unknowing*, thought to have been written in the fourteenth century by an anonymous English monk

When I first started writing, I spent a lot of time wringing my hands over the fact that I'd come to it so late. After a while I saw why I couldn't have written earlier: I didn't have anything to write *about*. I had no stance toward the world; no ground from which to proceed (and of course it didn't help that I was usually so hungover I could barely sit up). Not only were my neurotic depression and loneliness hardly the earth-shattering subjects I'd imagined; I had to replace them with the whole mystical, intellectual, scriptural, psychic bulwark of Christ.

That was only half the battle, though; the writing itself posed the real challenge. Probably like most folks who've ever written, my biggest mistake, especially at the beginning, was trying to sound smarter and more profound than I really am. Brenda Ueland's *If You Want to Write*, one of the best books I

know about writing, also has one of the funniest passages
I know about how hard it is to be simple and honest and true:

> When I was a staff writer on a magazine several years ago,
> and set to work on an article, I would write laboriously (and
> with what ennui! what struggle to pin my attention on it!)
> ten or twelve pages. I would realize then that I had just
> described very elaborately and with a great deal of rewriting
> and polishing, something that everybody knew already.
> With a sigh and as if throwing off a great weight, I would
> say to myself angrily:
> "What in thunder do you want to say?"
> "That women are too fat," my true self answered imme-
> diately and in a flash.
> "Well, put that down," I said to myself. And so I did, and
> it was right.

Almost any passage from Dostoyevsky displays a similar brac-
ing bluntness. Take this line from "White Nights": "[A]lthough
I've lived in Petersburg for eight years now, I haven't managed
to make a single friend." He could have rambled on about the
existential condition, or described his tortured childhood, or
railed against the shocking decline in contemporary morals, as
many lesser writers (such as myself) tend to do. Instead, when
the protagonist says he has no friends, I feel an instant kinship;
I think, *Here is someone who sees life as it is*, knowing I've gone
eight-year stretches with hardly a friend, too.

People sometimes say to me, "Oh, I could never write; I have

nothing to tell. Now, you—*you*'ve had an interesting life!" I
want to respond, "Oh, but like you, much of my life has consisted of depression, loneliness, boredom. Twenty years I spent
in dark barrooms, drinking cut-rate vodka and chain-smoking
with a bunch of fellow losers." Still, it's precisely in the losers
sitting around smoking cigarettes that the fun, the drama, the
conflict consists: nothing could be more charged with possibility
than a bunch of people in trouble, sitting around smoking
cigarettes.

Nothing could be more charged with meaning—about the
ways we comfort ourselves, about the way the things that keep
us alive also kill us—than, say, the bedside table of my friend
Fred. Fred is an ex–rodeo rider, ex-long-haul trucker, and ex–
skid row drunk who lives in a studio apartment off Sunset
Boulevard in a section of L.A called Silverlake, and we often
have long phone conversations describing in minute detail what
we ate for dinner, or our respective bedtime rituals, which, in
Fred's case, include setting up the table beside his mattress for
the long, possibly sleepless hours ahead. What have you got on
there? I once asked him.

You know, my water, my little candies. Butts.
Bottled water, or . . .
No, tap! You know me, I can't afford no bottled water.
What kind of glass? Do you put ice in it?
No ice, it hurts my teeth, I don't know, one a them glasses
    like jam comes in.
What kind of candies?

Cashews, Kit Kats.

Ya mean one big Kit Kat, or . . . ?

Nah, them little ones. You know, in a bag.

What kind of butts?

Marlboro 100s box, like always, I been tryin' to cut
   down. . . .

Now, where do buy all this stuff, Vons?

No! Big Five Liquor, right down here at the corner, *you* know,
   the guy who runs the place's a homo. . . .

People in trouble are always the interesting ones. In fact,
Jesus's whole ministry basically consisted of sitting around
with people who were in trouble, or sick, or misfits: eating,
drinking, telling stories. Speaking of stories, though, the trouble per se—the degradation, the scandal, the sin—is never
what's interesting: what's interesting is the movement *away*
from the sin; the transformation. Nothing is more boring than
degradation in and of itself, degradation that's sensationalized,
or glorified, or that's willfully wallowed in and bragged
about.

When I was drinking, I stayed stuck for two decades. Not
because I wanted to, but because I didn't know how to change,
I was afraid to change, I was in the grip of a compulsion that
was stronger than my will to change—so much stronger, in fact,
that it almost killed me. Still, when I decided to write the story,
the cockroach-ridden Boston loft, the sleeping around, the morning drinking in old men's bars weren't the point. The point was
the experience of a will deeply divided against itself; the discov-

ery that, no matter how low we sink, we're never beyond the reach of God's mercy.

That I came to writing at all is one of the blessings of my life, but that I'd come to it so late, as I said, meant that I was constantly trying to make up for lost time. What an ongoing surprise to find the spiritual path so glacially slow, and writing even slower! It's a difficult balance, to be driven—you have to be driven to write—and patient at the same time, and I was constantly straining to speed up, move faster, think things through: even in church, like the money changers in the temple (Matthew 21:12). I read a collection of interviews with the Cistercian monks in Vina, California, called *The Orchards of Perseverance*, and was fascinated to learn that, shortly after arriving, one guy, a real go-getter, had had a complete psychic breakdown. In order to perform his sweeping chores more quickly, he'd gotten the bright idea to tie together two brooms. The abbot had told him to go back to one broom, and for five years the guy had been barely able to function. If he couldn't be "productive," he literally didn't know who he was; he'd lost his identity. Five years! That gave me hope, because we are so trained to think things should happen quickly, when in fact it does seem to take years for any kind of psychic change, or work that's important to us, to come to fruition, to stay with it long enough for it to come to fruition is a feat. So when it comes to writing, instead of waiting, we give up, or rush into a different action. Or we compare ourselves to others and despair, or think we're freaks because we're so slow, or start gulping psychotropic meds.

Which I mention only because the thing to do, apparently, is continue to write—even though it seems as if you don't know how to do it, and are making no progress, and nobody's interested, and it's almost unbearably lonely. I once asked a woman who lives in the desert if she's ever gotten used to the heat. "I'm *accustomed* to it," she said carefully, and then added, "I chose to live here. I knew what I was getting into. If you choose to live in Alaska, you don't complain about the cold." If you choose to live in the tropics, you don't complain about the heat. And if you choose the writing life, I was reminded, you don't complain about the loneliness. You don't get to be all surprised and put upon because it's lonely.

When it comes to being published, I learned from my betters that you exercise the Christlike virtue of courtesy, defined by G. K. Chesterton as "the wedding of humility with dignity." Your attitude is that you can scarcely believe your good fortune—the bottomless honor it is to write at all, never mind to get to see the smallest thing in print. You realize it takes time and effort for people to come to a reading, or make an introduction, or write a note of support, and you thank people for it. You help the person who's coming up behind, because the people ahead, for no good reason, helped you. And when some shameful, obnoxious blowhard of a "fellow writer" tries to lord it over you, you look him square in the eye with a look that totally convicts him and totally forgives him, and say *sincerely*, "I'm so glad things are going well! Because a victory for one of us is a victory for all of us!" And you keep on writing.

With all that, it's an impossible line of work. Nobody but a pathological martyr, loner, alcoholic, drug addict, sexually conflicted, chronically depressed social misfit and/or religious fanatic could possibly stay with it long enough to write a single decent page. You have to be emotionally, spiritually, and physically fit; have to order your whole life around your writing schedule; have to develop the emotional hide of a rhinoceros to not simply die, as one dies under a stoning, beneath the endless barrage of insult, humiliation, rejection, disappointment, failure. And at the same time the only reason you do it at all, or can do it, or want to do it, is because of this incredibly tender heart, this heart you're a little ashamed of, that makes you different enough in the first place that writing is really your only refuge, your only means of enduring the world.

The closest I can come to describing how it feels for me is a passage from Kafka's "The Metamorphosis." As you may or may not know, Gregor Samsa is an office clerk who wakes one day to find himself turned into a giant cockroach. Torn between duty and disgust, Gregor's bourgeois family eventually relegates him to the secrecy of his musty bedroom. Starved, scorned, injured, increasingly weak, he's lying in bed one night when his parents and their three boarders gather in the living room to hear his sister play the violin. Gregor drags himself to the door, and in a last-gasp yearning to connect, ventures his dust-and-crumb-covered head inside the living room. "Was he an animal, that music moved him so?" he wonders—surely the question, or a variation of the question, artists down through the centuries have asked themselves as they struggle in obscurity, wondering whether their lives and work have meaning. That's the kind of tremulous, faintly pathetic feeling you develop about yourself and your work. But maybe just because it's so tremulous, because you let yourself be vulnerable, it has a curious strength that makes it impervious to setback. As Christ said, "See, I am sending you out like sheep in the midst of wolves; so be wise as serpents and innocent as doves" (Matthew 10:16), and I don't know a place that applies more aptly than to a life that's devoted to writing, or the arts.

When I first heard the phrase "communion of saints," I figured it referred to that rarefied group of superpious people who had been, say, torn apart by lions, or roasted over a gridiron, or had their breasts chopped off rather than yield their virginity. In fact, as the Catechism explains, it comprises the entire Catholic Church: "We believe in the communion of all the faithful of Christ, those who are pilgrims on earth, the dead who are being purified, and the blessed in heaven, and we believe that in this communion, the merciful love of God and his saints is always [attentive] to our prayers" (section 962).

I found the idea that the dead could be called upon for help deeply appealing. Most of the dead people I felt closest to were writers, and I soon developed my own personal communion of saints: Kafka, Flannery O'Connor, Dostoyevsky, Emily Dickinson, Chekhov, Hank Williams. As far as I knew, the only practicing Catholics in the group were Dostoyevsky and O'Connor, but that didn't bother me in the least. In my book, anyone who could write "I'm So Lonesome I Could Cry"—and sing it the way Hank Williams did—had definitely grasped the essence of Christ.

Many of the writers I admired had suffered from or died early of debilitating diseases—TB, alcoholism, lupus—but when it came to their work (and, in some cases, for all their supposed neuroses), they displayed an astounding, warriorlike tenacity. Kafka had penned two of his finest works—"A Hunger Artist" and *The Castle*—while dying of tuberculosis. Nothing had kept him from working, not the collapsed lungs that made him feel like he was breathing splinters of glass, not the tormented nerves that had plagued him all his life. "God doesn't want me to write, but I—I must . . . and there's more anguish in it than you can imagine," he wrote to a friend.

Dennis Potter, the late, brilliant British TV writer, suffered his entire career from psoriatic arthropathy, a disfiguring and excruciatingly painful condition that—with the help of gargantuan quantities of alcohol, nicotine, caffeine, and morphine—fueled a streak of creativity I could only view with the deepest awe and respect. He wore pajamas under his clothes to contain the clouds of flaking skin, turned in scripts splattered with blood and cortisone cream, and, when his hand was too crabbed with arthritis to hold a pen, strapped the pen on and continued writing anyway. Upon being diagnosed with inoperable cancer, he put his affairs in order and established a grueling, nonstop work schedule that enabled him not only to finish the last two works he'd planned but to go on and write more.

Swollen with cortisone, her joints crippled, novelist and short-story writer Flannery O'Connor worked fiercely through years of the lupus that would kill her at the age of thirty-nine. When her mother urged her to go to Lourdes, she reluctantly did, writing afterward to a friend, "I prayed there for the novel I was working on, not for my bones, which I care about less. . . ." Three weeks before dying, she wrote to a friend, "I'm still in bed but I climb out of it into the typewriter about 2 hours every morning." Two weeks before: "I'm still puttering on my story that I thought I'd finished but not long at a time. I go across the room and I'm exhausted." Nine days before, she learned that her story "Revelation" had won first place in the O. Henry competition.

No matter how bad things got during my drinking years, I always managed to have a stack of library books. With the instincts of a homing pigeon, I'd make my hungover way from my West End "loft" (loft implies some kind of artistic creativity, but the only thing I ever created there was a giant mess—of my life) through Government Center to Tremont Street, across the Common and Public Gardens, past the Ritz, the Arlington Street Church, and up Boylston Street to the Boston Public Library, with its Renaissance-palazzo stone facade and arched windows and tiled roof. Inside, I trolled the stacks, hands atremble at the sight of a fresh Graham Greene or Henry James; the smell of paper, ink, bindings as primal as the smell of sex. Books are inherently life-affirming, incarnational; and heading home with a fresh haul, I held mine close, hurrying them back to my apartment to be savored in privacy.

Books saved my life—literally kept me from killing myself—and now I know it was because so many people were willing to burn out their lives in front of a page trying to get it right. People whose goal wasn't to sound smarter or more profound than the rest of us, but to show us what it means to be human. People who set out not to sensationalize their pain, but to shed light on ours. People who didn't set themselves above the world, but were part of the world, and loved the world and suffered for it, and made art of their suffering. These are the heroes I look up to, whose feet I hope to sit at one day, whom I hope to have a chance to thank for their stories that sustained and comforted me, their hard, hard work, their example. Maybe fetch them a glass of water, a bedpan, a pill. If I'm lucky—polish their crowns.

CHAPTER 15

"But"—people say to me—"if you consider that apart from the fulfill-
ment of the Christian teaching there is no reasonable life, and if you
love that reasonable life, why do you not fulfill the commands?" I
reply that I am a horrible creature and deserve blame and contempt
for not fulfilling them. . . . Blame *me*, and not the path I tread and
show to those who ask me where in my opinion the road lies! If I
know the road home and go along it drunk, staggering from side to
side—does that make the road along which I go a wrong one?

—Leo Tolstoy

Tim and I had gotten married without ever having held a single
conversation about "issues" or "boundaries." We loved each
other; what could come up that wouldn't work itself out? A man
I worked with at the time gently prophesied, "The things you'll
argue about are money and housework." I remember thinking
with pity that his marriage must be terribly shallow if he and
his wife allowed those niggling matters to come between
them.

Now that we'd been married 14 years, I knew better. When
we'd first gotten together, I'd still equated intimacy with sex. I
didn't know that real intimacy would have meant talking not
only about money and housework but about our fears, our

desires, our personal histories. With a couple of sober years, I'd *wanted* to settle down, I'd *wanted* to be faithful—which, with my history in the bars, was at least a start (not to mention a minor miracle). I'd instinctively understood that marriage is a sacrament, that within the constraint of marriage is freedom, that the relationship was larger than either of us. I'd made a lifelong vow and I meant to keep it. But with all that, I hadn't even begun to deal with my ancient wounds: my terrible fear of rejection, my deep conviction that I was unworthy of love, my borderline panic at the prospect of being abandoned.

At the time, we were living on the North Shore of Boston. We'd eloped to Nantucket and I remember looking down at my $35 plain gold band those first few years and thinking, a bit smugly, that marriage wasn't about fancy rings, it was about fidelity and loyalty and sticking with each other through thick and thin. Which is true enough, in its way, but I didn't realize that to keep a vow of that magnitude requires help. The union needs to be consecrated to the service of, and before, some larger community—which is one of the reasons people have public weddings and, often, eventually, children. I think both of us secretly wanted children but for various reasons were too afraid to, so we agreed up front we didn't want them. Obviously we weren't bound to have children, but we should have at least had an absorbing, challenging, and life-enhancing shared goal.

Unfortunately we did not, with the result that pretty quickly we started having arguments about—lo and behold—housework and money. When I began working as a lawyer, for example, I was thrilled to be making a good salary for the first time in my

life; I gladly spent thousands of dollars buying appliances, kitch-
enware, and furnishing the house. After a while, though, I
noticed Tim wasn't nearly that forthcoming. He was working as
a carpenter, and therefore not making nearly as much money as
I was, but still, I began to wonder: *Why didn't he ever go out and
buy a vacuum, or a gas grill, or at least take me out to eat?* Chores
were a problem, too: I was pulling my weight, and I assumed a
person of even nominal courtesy, good sportsmanship, and common sense would naturally, instinctively, pull his. Instead, he
seemed to come to *expect* me to clean, shop, and cook; or worse,
to imagine I enjoyed these odious tasks.

Another person—more mature, less afraid—would have perhaps tried to talk these things out, but at the time, direct
communication was a concept almost utterly beyond my ken.
In retrospect, I guess I hoped *he'd* communicate, or that it would
happen by osmosis, or that sex would take care of it. The truth
was I was terrified that if I asked for anything, or if we had a
conflict, or if I wasn't perfect, he'd leave. So instead of admitting
I felt afraid of not being loved, and afraid of being taken advan-
tage of, I made a unilateral, private decision to be entirely
responsible for myself—emotionally, spiritually, socially, financially. The way I let my husband in on this was announcing that
henceforth we were going to split our finances exactly down the
middle. Every month I did the bills and every month I began to
present him with an itemized tally, accurate down to the penny,
of the half he owed. It seemed only fair to eventually apply the
same principle to everything else: to expect him to do his half—
and silently resent him when he didn't—of watering the plants,
scrubbing the sink, reserving plane tickets when we went on

vacation. Being a lawyer did come in handy for one thing: the airtight case I was able to build against my husband. I had it down to Roman numeral XIV, subparagraph c, section 328.7492. It was simple: I always did my share, and he never did his. No jury could convict me.

We'd been married five years when I converted to Catholicism and he became a Buddhist. Whatever other benefits our respective paths may have brought us, the fact that they were different paths allowed us to shut each other out even more. Every morning he hauled out the bench he'd made for himself, faced the wall in a corner of the living room, and meditated for half an hour: I came to regard the sight of his ramrod-straight back as a big LEAVE ME ALONE. I got the impression he felt the same way every time I went to Mass (always by myself, of course), or—rather pointedly, I see in retrospect—cracked open yet another of my religious books. For much of my marriage I was curled up on the couch reading *The Cloister Walk* or *Convents of Southern France* or *Notable Hermits* (then I'd wonder why we never had sex). When I wasn't reading, I was planning solo trips: retreats to monasteries, sojourns to the desert. Another dream was to go on pilgrimage; at one point I was determined to purchase a rucksack and staff and walk across the Pyrenees.

Still, we continued to cook, hike, hang out, and enjoy each other's company. We understood that the basic purpose of marriage is to enrich each other and then go out and enrich the world, and we both continued to do our part, sometimes separately, sometimes together, to "help our neighbor." But all the while we were growing further apart; we were living lives that were parallel, not entwined; that intersected less and less. We never "fought": that would have been too scary for either of us. We just retreated to our separate corners.

For a long time I wouldn't even consider divorce. For a few agonized years I sat on the fence: *Should I leave or shouldn't I? Could the marriage be saved or couldn't it? Was it* possible *it could end?* And then came a crisis. I'd gone away for a month to a writer's residency, in the mountains outside L.A., and one weekend Tim came out to visit. The chaparral was bone dry, and a fire watch was in effect all over the mountain. We were sitting outside my cabin after dinner when Tim lit a match to burn some sage we'd picked. "Oh, honey," I piped up, "we're not allowed to have any kind of fires out here. They're gonna yell at us if they see that." Whatever it was in me that he hated—my bossiness, or that I was away at this place to write and he'd come to visit and I was *still* going to shut him out—all came to a head around this seemingly small incident: his entire body stiffened and went cold with rage. We barely talked the rest of the night, he took off early the next morning, and for the first time I allowed myself to think, *I don't know if I can do this anymore.*

I sensed that God loves a long marriage. I knew the Church frowned on divorce. I knew the Eucharistic ramifications of divorce (if I married again without having the first marriage annulled, I'd be bound to refrain from taking the Eucharist). I took my marriage vows seriously, I took my vows as a Catholic even more seriously, and when I consulted my Catechism, I read: "Divorce is a grave offense against the natural law. It claims to break the contract, to which the spouses freely consented, to live with each other till death. Divorce does injury to the covenant of salvation, of which sacramental marriage is the sign. . . . Divorce is immoral because it introduces disorder into the family and into society. . . ." (sections 2384–2385).

I couldn't have agreed more. The Catholic view of marriage is that its purpose is the bearing and raising of children; it's not just so that two people can have sex, or human company, or a best friend, as good as those things are. The relationship is bigger than either of the people in it; its aim is the greater, common good. I'd understood that going in: marriage was a way I had wanted to contribute to the world, been prepared to sacrifice, even, in order to contribute. Though we hadn't had children ourselves, in a sense I'd stayed married for *other* people's children. I'd taken a vow for life, and personal integrity demanded that if I were planning to break it, it should be with a view of increasing my hardship, not diminishing it. Leaving a marriage should be a holy sacrifice, not an escape; a movement toward authenticity, not ease. But if I did leave, would that be the case with me?

I didn't know, and at the same time I was nearing the breaking point. Every second Tim and I were together I felt the juggernaut of his silent, deeply violent hostility bearing down on me. I remember thinking I would rather he'd hit me: overt violence at least has heat and blood in it, but such coldness crushed my soul. I suggested counseling a few times, and he balked, and that made me feel more unloved, unacknowledged, unseen than ever. One night I had a complete meltdown. I was frantic and unnerved; we were sitting in the living room, and even though he wasn't even doing anything, I started shrieking, "You are BULLYING me, you are BULLYING me, don't you

DARE BULLY me." He'd never seen me like that; it was a cataclysmic moment; I think something broke in him then, too.

Right after that, for the first time in my life, I started going
to a shrink. I was on the verge of being suicidal; I just could not
see a way out. I saw this woman three or four times, and, oddly,
I hardly talked about my marriage at all: I talked about my
mother. Still, this somehow helped me figure out that if it came
down to killing myself or getting divorced, God would prefer I
got divorced. On the fourth or fifth visit I announced, "I'm leaving my husband," and the shrink said, "Really! I didn't even
know you were married."

For weeks after, my brain was awhirl. *Was I nothing but a
quitter? Didn't staying in difficult situations build character?* I
went and spoke to the priest I'm closest to, my beloved Father
Terry. He referred me to a passage from St. Paul which reads in
part, "And if any woman has a husband who is an unbeliever,
and he consents to live with her, she should not divorce him.
For the unbelieving husband is made holy through his wife, and
the unbelieving wife is made holy through her husband. . . . But
if the unbelieving partner separates, let it be so; in such a case
the brother or sister is not bound. It is to peace that God has
called you. . . ." (1 Corinthians 7:13–16).

Tim was consenting to live with me in body, not spirit: but
did that constitute a legitimate reason to leave? More to the
point, I was so convinced that marriage was an, if not *the*, arena
in which my character was supposed to be hammered out.
Where I was supposed to develop! What about my health insurance, someone to pay half the bills, my day-in, day-out
companion? "Are you able to drink the cup that I drink?" Jesus

asked his disciples (Mark 10:38): the cup of loneliness, the cup of change? My whole idea of and relationship with God—what he wanted from me, the course my path was meant to follow—was getting shaken up, just as it had when I'd changed careers, and gotten breast cancer.

When we separated at last, Tim moved out, leaving me the apartment. Far from bringing the relief I'd hoped for, this was only the beginning of yet another long, painful process. I'd wanted to separate, I'd come to believe it was right, I felt good about finally having made the decision, but I was still unprepared for the ensuing trauma. I hadn't expected to feel so afraid: of not being able to take care of myself, of dying alone. I hadn't expected to feel the loss of status, the poverty—financial, social, emotional, psychological, physical, even spiritual—of a previously married woman without a man. I hadn't expected such a profound sense of failure that I hadn't loved as well or as much as I longed to: to love this person who was decent, kind, faithful, in many ways giving, and whom I'd come in many ways to bitterly resent. The real danger in divorce is the hardening of heart, which always disrupts the social order. Over the course of 16 years, mine had hardened more than I cared to admit.

It was a year before I could bring myself to file for divorce; another year before it was finalized. Then, like a good Catholic, I went about getting an annulment. Tim balked and refused to cooperate, but I hardly resisted at all. I hadn't cheated on him, or bolted at the first sign of trouble, but I *had* broken a covenant with another human being and with God. So I understood that the intent behind the annulment process wasn't to punish, or induce guilt, but to corroborate that our acts are eternal, that the bonds we form in marriage are sacred. I needed to acknowledge that sacrament, come to terms with why mine went wrong, and allow the Church to prepare me in the event I decided to enter into the sacrament again. I needed to be obedient to a process that, in its somewhat clumsy way, accorded the fullest possible significance to the human heart, sense of trust, sexual capacity, and conscience.

That's not to say I didn't go into it with a certain amount of dread. My biggest (of course, selfish) fear was that I'd go through the whole ordeal and the annulment wouldn't be granted. I also worried that claiming a "grave defect" had existed from the start would be hypocritical. I imagined being summoned before a tribunal and questioned by a mean-spirited nun. I was afraid of being subjected to an outlandish invasion of privacy. Instead, the whole process took place on paper (and cost four hundred bucks), and answering the questions they asked turned out to be unexpectedly helpful. Getting my own emotional, sexual, and spiritual history—as well as the emotional, sexual, and spiritual history of the marriage—down on paper helped me see that there really had been a defect, if not several, from the start. It helped me see the irony—and humor—in the fact that while I'd been supposedly so intent on the "spiritual path," I'd been harboring such pettiness, such irritation, such almost murderous rage. It helped me begin to wish my incessant thought hadn't been *Does he care about me?* but *How can I show I care about* him?

I knew I didn't have the courage or honesty to sort things through on my own; I had to ask God for help. When I did, I saw I'd made two major changes during the course of the marriage.

188 | *Heather King*

I'd started writing (which entailed quitting my fairly lucrative job as a lawyer), and I'd converted to Catholicism (which Tim, obviously, had not): two areas that had come increasingly to be the ground of my existence, and that he couldn't share in; he'd felt shut out by both. I began to feel more and more sympathy for him there, because I *had* shut him out. I needed a certain kind of solitude to write, and I needed a certain kind of solitude in which to reflect and contemplate, but I could have somehow included him in my solitude, held him in it: I never had. I'd always thought of myself as "putting up" with him, but now I realized how much he'd put up with me: my compulsion to control, my anxiety, my wildly fluctuating moods. I saw it hadn't been his "fault," it had just been a very difficult situation—for both of us. I began to feel how terribly, terribly hurtful it must have been for him. I discuss my feelings easily; I write about them; I keep a journal. He was a private, stoic New Englander; like many men, he may have viewed showing his emotions as a sign of weakness. So he had kept it all in, all that time, with nobody to share it with, least of all me.

It had been easy for me to admit I'd nitpicked and kept score: I'd already apologized to him for that. But in the weeks that followed I came to see I had never really admitted, even to myself, that the scorekeeping had been precipitated by a deeper, underlying grudge; an entrenched hurt. I'd never had the courage to ask him, but one thing I'd wanted more than anything: I'd always wanted him to build me a house. He was a carpenter; he helped everyone else on their houses; why hadn't he wanted to build me one? But how could I have said it out loud? It was so *Cosmo* girl, so corny! Plus I'd had some idea of protecting his feelings; I hadn't wanted to impugn his manhood by implying he wasn't *able* to take care of me. That's what I'd told myself, anyway. But the real fear was that if I asked, he'd look at me in disbelief and say, "Are you crazy? I don't care enough about you to build you any *house*." I'd preferred not to know, and to assume, because it never happened, that he hadn't cared. I'd been mad at him the whole time for not doing something I'd never told him I wanted. I'd never really opened up to him, the whole time we were married, and then I'd held it against him. I thought I'd be loved by being strong, by carrying my own weight, by not needing anything. I'd never understood we are loved by being vulnerable.

Not long after, I read a reflection by Dorothy Day, founder of the Catholic Worker: that because God transcends time, we can pray for dead people as if they were still alive; we can pray for God to be close to them with respect to problems or illnesses or crises they had when they were still alive, and the prayer some-how helps them with those problems they had while they were still alive. I thought of all the thousands of times I'd washed the dishes resentfully, shopped resentfully, cooked, cleaned, planned trips resentfully, and I thought, *Let those things have been done with love, let them have been done with the purest, most unadul-terated love, the love that we long for with all our hearts and that HE SO DESERVES.* I don't mean I was trying to wish away the hardness of heart; I don't believe in magical thinking. But maybe my hard-heartedness could be transformed; maybe my heart could be softened toward him not only now, but in retrospect—for the whole time we were married.

Tim had moved back to New Hampshire, and we were still talking, though I wouldn't exactly describe it as warm. Then one day out of the blue I got a letter from him saying, among other things, "I'm sorry for the hell I put you through." That's exactly how I'd come to think of the last three or four years of our marriage: he'd put me through hell. But the minute *he* said it, and I felt *his* guilt, remorse, sorrow, sense of failure, everything in me melted. I thought, *It wasn't hell. You didn't put me through hell, we both tried the very best we could....*

We hurt people just by being who we are, by being impenetrable and mysterious—but isn't the real miracle that, with the complexities of the human heart, any two people ever get together at all? We held hands for part of the journey, and I'll never regret that. Maybe the marriage, in the fullest sense of the sacrament, never quite came into being, but something did that was vital and bore fruit and mattered. I still haven't quite worked it through: divorce may be one of those things that never quite heals. But I'm grateful—for him. That he's found someone else. For the time that was us.

CHAPTER 16

Truth nailed upon the cross compels nobody, oppresses no one; it must be accepted and confessed freely; its appeal is addressed to free spirits.

—Nicholas Berdyaev, Russian theologian and religious philosopher

I am always amazed at people who, when disaster strikes—tsunamis, Hurricane Katrina, 9/11—say they're so affected they can't sleep at night. I want to say, Really? I slept fine. If I were capable of being so affected by the deaths of people I don't know, I wouldn't have been able to sleep since hearing of the AIDS epidemic in Africa, the famine in North Korea, the genocide in the Sudan, or, for that matter, the Holocaust. The tsunami hits and people are all indignant—they're like, How *could* it? Where was God? What shall we do? And my feeling is, What do you mean what shall we do? Have you not heard that people are *dying all the time*? People die every day; all over the world thousands and thousands of people are dying. They're dying in convalescent homes down the street from our apartments: when's the last time we visited one of them? They're dying in mental institutions, they've been rotting away for years: when's the last time we flocked to the Red Cross for that? They're dying in car crashes, being electrocuted in their kitchens, falling through the ice on their first pair of skates. Isn't the real question why anybody dies at all? What keeps me up at night—or should—are the abortions I've had.

I hesitate to even have an opinion on, say, the hurricane in New Orleans; to purport to put myself in the shoes of, say, a father, crouching on the roof with his family, watching the water rise and ruin everything he owns. I've never had that particular experience—I've never owned enough money to buy or even, with the exception of two years, rent a house. On the other hand, every human being above the age of five has experienced the fear of abandonment, the sense that the world is a terrifying, alien place, the conviction that there's no justice, no reason, no God. This is not to in any way purport to understand the suffering of the people, or any one person, in New Orleans. But it is to say that the only way I can begin to understand it *is* through one person. I can't get my mind around collective suffering and this may not be only for lack of compassion. As C. S. Lewis observed in *The Problem of Pain*, "There is no such thing as a sum of suffering, for no one suffers it. When we have reached the maximum that a single person can suffer, we have, no doubt, reached something very horrible, but we have reached all the suffering there can ever be in the universe. The addition of a million fellow sufferers adds no more pain."

It not only doesn't add more pain, it tells me nothing about pain itself, nor the strange fact that whatever pain we undergo seems in large part to form who we are. The suffering I've had myself I wouldn't wish on my worst enemy and yet I'd fight to the death for my right to have had the experiences and worked them through. I distrust the kind of "compassion" that wants to rush in and clean everything up, the "compassion" that wants to clone out imperfections, that wants to put the old folks out of "their" (read "whoever's taking care of them") misery, that thinks poverty can be fixed by "policies" and "programs." In fact, it *can't* be fixed, if for no other reason than that we are all the poor: "You always have the poor with you," as Christ said (John 12:8). That doesn't mean I don't have an obligation to help out any and every way I can. He also said, "Just as you did it to one of the least of these who are members of my family, you did it to me" (Matthew 25:40). But the way to help out seems to be the one-on-one, often awkward, face-to-face encounter—the one that has a chance of influencing and affecting and transforming not only the person I'm "helping," but me.

Maybe it's because suffering is so bottomlessly mysterious that I'm nervous when I start getting proprietary about it. It's obnoxious to think I know how bad anyone else's suffering is, but it's just as obnoxious to think mine is worse than anyone else's. One person's pain can't be compared to another's. As Victor Frankl noted in *Man's Search for Meaning* (in a strange choice of metaphor, considering he'd been in the Nazi death camps): "If a certain quantity of gas is pumped into an empty chamber, it will fill the chamber completely and evenly, no matter how big the chamber. Thus suffering completely fills the human soul and conscious mind, no matter whether the suffering is great or little. Therefore the 'size' of human suffering is absolutely relative."

Maybe the most obnoxious thing of all is to imagine that I could or would have arranged the world better. I collude in the sorrows of the world, in the things I do, and the things I fail to do: day in, day out. On the one hand I'm not nearly compassion-ate enough, and on the other I'm too compassionate, or rather I mistake nosiness and thinking I know best for compassion, then go about trying to subtly or not so subtly manage other peoples' affairs; to fix them. As everyone knows by now, compassion means "suffering with," and it is a discipline that seems to be cultivated slowly, painstakingly, at great sacrifice, and over a long period of time. Mostly it seems to be cultivated through great suffering of my own and the realization that I understand almost nothing of the way the world works, and would do better trying to fix a few of the trillions of things that are wrong with me rather than trying to fix someone else.

The best I can figure is that God doesn't cause us to suffer, but he doesn't prevent us from suffering. He's created a world where suffering is possible and given us his only son as the means to bear, subsume, transcend it. Not on the off chance we'll find redemption, but because in a world without suffering—without consequences for our actions—free will would have no meaning; without suffering, we would have no reason, opportunity, or motive to love. I don't believe God wills that I get cancer (and that you maybe don't), though I do notice he created us with bodies that are subject to disease, accident, and aging, and become absorbed in wondering why. I don't believe God killed the other person in the plane crash and saved me, but since it so happens that I was spared, the least I can do is give thanks, and spend the rest of my time on earth trying to help out a little.

It's not so much suffering I don't understand, actually, as why *I* have to suffer. I can't quite believe that I and my loved ones aren't immune; that we don't win points for good behavior. This was Job's dilemma: why do bad things happen to good people? One answer may be that I'm not nearly as good as I think. I spend my life in the pursuit of happiness, for example, and then I'm shocked—SHOCKED!—that, for instance, the black people were left behind after Hurricane Katrina. What are the chances, really, I have to ask myself right now, that if a flood were threatening my apartment, before getting the hell into my car and out of the city as fast as humanly possible, I'd mosey down to Central L.A. and make sure the black folk were out first? When's the last time I offered a homeless person anything more than a buck and a shamed half-smile? How can I abort my own child, then purport to abhor the mind that would plan 9/11? It's not the same thing, but it is the same principle: I'm more valuable than you; you're in the way; one of us has to go. God hasn't been, or isn't, responsible for war, pillaging, rape, torture, prisons, the Inquisition, the Holocaust, racial, ethnic, or gender discrimination, suicide bombings, nuclear weapons, global warming, the failure or refusal to share our food, shelter, clothing, education, medical care, time, money, prayers, and heart with each other: people are. Isn't the real question most of the time not where was God, but where was I?

I think the best answer to the question Where is God? came to Elie Wiesel as he watched a ten-year-old boy "with the face of an angel" being hanged in Auschwitz for a breach of camp rules. Where is God? Wiesel asked, and a voice answered, *Where? Here He is. He has been hanged on these gallows.*

Wiesel took that to mean God was dead. But to believe that Christ is God incarnate is to believe that any violence we suffer he suffers as well—that he does get hanged with us, does get raped with us, does die with us. But it is also to believe he rises with us—and it has always seemed to me a deep and shattering mystery that when Christ appeared to his disciples after the Resurrection, he still bore the wounds. One of the things this seems to say is that our suffering counts. Our wounds aren't wiped away, as in a fairy tale: our bodies and souls bear their marks into eternity. Maybe that's how we'll recognize, or classify, or take joy in each other after we die, because maybe then we'll see how our suffering helped someone else, or perhaps saved another from suffering.

Another thing it seems to say is that we are useful here on earth even in—perhaps especially in—our wounds: physical, emotional, spiritual. I tend to think I know God's "plan" for people: of course if the guy's a falling-down drunk he "should" get sober; of course if the person's sick she should get better. But maybe some people are just as useful, or even more so, drunk than sober. That's not to say we boozehounds should just give up and start swilling Thunderbird 24/7—no, we have to try with everything in us to stop. But if we can't, maybe God uses even our illnesses, our compulsions, the defects we can't fix no matter how hard we try, for the greater good. As for the wounds other people inflict upon us—maybe he uses those most of all.

Maybe the ones who suffer more bear it for the rest of us who are too weak and cowardly to bear it. Five years after 9/11, excerpts from the 1,613 emergency phone calls made from the World Trade Center that morning were released to the public. Melissa Doi, thirty-two years old, called from the eighty-third floor of the south tower. When the operator answered, Doi responded, "Holy Mary, mother of God," and continued, "there's no one here yet and the floor's completely engulfed. We are on the floor and we can't breathe and it's very, very hot." The operator tried to calm her down, but a few minutes later Doi panicked: "I'm going to die, aren't I?" she asked. "No, no, no," the operator replied. "I'm going to die," Doi repeated. "Say your prayers," the operator advised. "Oh God, it's so hot. I'm burning up," Doi replied. Several minutes later, the line on her end went silent. And here's the thing, really, in a way—one of the very few things we have to hold on to: the operator continued to speak to her for another 20 minutes, "soothingly," according to a *Los Angeles Times* article, "repeating Doi's name over and over, calling her 'dear.'"

Holy Mary, mother of God. Say your prayers, ma'am. Oh God, it's so hot, I'm burning up. . . . Oh, Osama bin Laden (and let's remember there's a little Osama bin Laden in the best of us), if you were sitting beside this beautiful young woman—because all young women are beautiful, all people are beautiful—if you could see the part in her hair, feel her breath on your hand, maybe you could have seen that if one of us is hurt, we're all hurt. That whatever hurt has been done to you, this could never set it right. That it's not making fire in the sky and blowing up towers that make you a man. It's love: the kind of love where you'd offer yourself up to be incinerated so that someone else wouldn't have to be. The kind of love where you'd let yourself be nailed to a cross rather than order a brother to kill himself. The kind of love that says someone's name into the darkness and the silence, over and over again, to say that Melissa Doi's life, her death, were not in vain. Twenty minutes, over and over, into the darkness, the silence, into what I have to believe ascended to, was heard, echoed through the farthest reaches of the cosmos. Twenty minutes, over and over, one beating heart to another, through the sky above New York, through the heavens, through eternity, until one stopped beating—and the other kept calling out to her anyway.

CHAPTER 17

We are not a people who think we are better. We are not an elite. We are people who are poor, but who have been drawn together by God and put their trust in God. That is what a kingdom community is all about: a community that knows it has been called by God in all its poverty and weakness, and that God is love.

—Jean Vanier

I live alone, but a big part of my life is the communities in which I participate: the people into whose hands, day by day, I deliver myself and my soul. I think it has to be a big part of any life, and in particular, of the Catholic life. One community consists of my family: my mother, seven far-flung brothers and sisters, assorted nieces and nephews. Another comprises people I meet in person, on the phone, or online through my work. But mostly, I have the fellow addicts and alcoholics into whose midst I stumbled 19 years ago and who, to my everlasting surprise and gratitude, haven't yet kicked me out.

In community, I discover my task is to play my part, however small, in the ongoing drama of creation. I learn, over and over, to pray one of the most succinct and best prayers I know: bless them; change me. I learn I'm no better than anyone else, but I'm no worse either. Still, it's nice to have someone to look up to—a fellow alcoholic, a fellow Catholic. For me, that's Father (actually Monsignor) Terry Richey. Terry's official title is director of substance abuse ministry for the Archdiocese of Los Angeles but, in or out of his job, all he does is help alcoholics anyway. Terry's own run with alcohol himself resulted in 24 "aversion treatments" and 7 stints at rehab (the last of which finally "took"), and though he's a cradle Catholic and a by-the-book diocesan priest, his spirituality has been largely shaped by the death-and-resurrection experience of having gotten, and continuing to stay, sober. He hasn't had a drink or a drug in 35 years, and once I'd gotten to know him, I couldn't help thinking he'd spent the entire time developing an interesting, thought-provoking, helpful, Christ-based take on just about every important imaginable question: what's hell? Do I have a moral obligation *not* to try to get out of jury duty? Is masturbation really a mortal sin?

Victorian poet Coventry Patmore observed, of the difference between normal people and saints, "The saint does everything that any other decent person does, only somewhat better and with a totally different motive." That's Terry. He makes himself available to everyone (and I mean *everyone*), but he's private. When I'm with him, he makes me feel alive and hopeful and acknowledged—and when it's time to part, he leaves, without clinging or regret. He entered the seminary at 14, and for 42 years has been praying the Divine Office, serving at various parishes, leading retreats, ministering to the newly born, the sick, the imprisoned, the dying. That kind of discipline molds and tempers a person, the quiet fruit of which is that people change around him. He claims to have an enormous ego—I once asked, "Now don't be modest, but what if we got some of

your delightful and well-thought-out spirituality down on paper!
Wouldn't that be fun? Have you ever thought of anything like
that?" He replied dryly, "I never think of anything else," but I
swear you'd never know it.

One huge gift of the Church is the rhythm of the liturgical year:
the seven-week darkness of Lent; the in-between months of "Ordinary Time"; the four weeks before Christmas, known as Advent.
Advent and Lent have acquired particular significance for me
because they've come to mean Father Terry and our Wednesday-
night ragtag group of spiritual seekers. A few of us are Catholic
converts, a few are of other denominations, a few aren't "religious"
at all. Conny, Judy, Mike, and I are alcoholics. Glenn had a small
problem going to the baths. Joan struggled for years with bulimia.
Which makes it just right, since addiction of one kind or another
is the state of so many people in the Gospels.

I've been coming to these gatherings for seven or eight years,
but Terry and some of the others have been getting together for
around sixteen. Anyone's welcome and it's a rare night that a
stray friend, visitor, or lost soul doesn't wander in. The tone is
specifically Christ-centered: the general format is that we
read that upcoming Sunday's Liturgy of the Word, Terry does
a 15-minute reflection, and then we go around the table and each
of us gives our own little take on it, or some other spiritual
observation/reflection, or whatever else is on our minds.

The discussion, however, usually isn't so much about Christ
per se as it is about the awakening that comes from hitting bottom with an addiction and, by some mysterious grace, climbing
out. We've all experienced it to one degree or another, and Terry

has a wonderful way of articulating how this slow, ongoing awakening looks. He talks about our deeply misguided desire to be saved through excellence—but not in an arrogant way: how we want to be spontaneous yet profound, highly intelligent yet down-to-earth, well-balanced yet passionate, dignified but self-deprecating, physically fit, good-looking, calm in the face of tragedy, suave in the face of heartbreak, and with really, really good skin. He talks about how we're so afraid of being judged, and how—when we get sober, or we come into the church, or we come back to the human race in whatever way we've come back—we're judged welcome. He talks about how every act counts, everything we say, think, do "registers."

All ethical, loving behavior, as Terry points out, is an experience of thanksgiving. Grace always opens a path to love, to joy. In that context, "rules" like not committing adultery and the indissolubility of marriage don't seem like sacrifices: they're the natural outgrowth of that joy. "You're in this situation of mutually self-giving love," he says, "and you wouldn't *think* of cheating: it'd just be so . . . it'd wreck *everything*." Or he'll be talking about the Crucifixion, saying, "And when you're on fire with love, of *course* you're going to give up everything for the kid, or for your brothers and sisters, of *course* you don't mind dying." I'll be following along, nodding my head, thinking *Unh-unh, unh-unh, no of course I don't mind dying,* and then suddenly I'll be caught short and think: *I* don't? On the other hand, there's a danger in thinking God's will is to suffer, to martyr ourselves: as Terry points out from time to time during Lent, Christ had a rich, full life—and then three really bad days.

I enjoy traveling this journey of inner darkness with a group, and Lent generates myriad other interesting topics—the temptation in the desert, the permutations of fasting. One year we spent all seven weeks on *With Burning Hearts,* a series of reflections by Henri Nouwen about the incident after the Crucifixion when Christ appeared to his disciples on the road to Emmaus (Luke 24:13–35). At first, they thought he was a stranger. But he walked with them all day, sharing his spiritual insights, and when he was at the table with them that night, "he took bread, blessed and broke it, and gave it to them. Then their eyes were opened, and they recognized him; and he vanished from their sight": a phenomenon to which anyone who's ever experienced the maddening ephemerality of spiritual connection can attest.

Advent has its own rich and stirring liturgy, permeated with a sense of wonder, expectancy, and hope. "Prepare the way of the Lord," John the Baptist cries out in the wilderness; "make his paths straight" (Luke 3:4), and in the coming four weeks, in our way, it's as if we prepare a room, or a womb, to receive Christ. We talk about how new life, and real love, seem to be always accompanied by pain. We talk about the fact that Mary and Joseph were refugees, and how "No Room at the Inn" could be the title for the story of our collective psyche. Father Terry always says the five o'clock Vigil Mass on Christmas Eve at St. Basil's, and most of us show up. Part of me these nights is forever back in my New Hampshire childhood, at the candlelight ceremony at the Congregational Church that was right across the street from our house. The familiar readings are like a lullaby: "Behold, the virgin shall conceive and bear a son, and they shall name

204 | *Heather King*

him Emmanuel," "A decree went out from Caesar Augustus," "She wrapped him in swaddling clothes and laid him in a manger." Terry has a whole take on, and often manages to work into his homily, the fact that Christ came into the world as a baby, and that in its helplessness and vulnerability, a baby throws everything out of whack. We don't think about what it can do for us or how it makes us feel; we instinctively try to figure out what it wants or needs even if the baby itself doesn't. And for those of us who aren't "lucky" enough to be parents, if we're *really* lucky, someone will come into our life who is so desperate, so incredibly damaged and difficult, so needy we won't be able to avoid them; they'll blow our lives apart just like a baby does, and teach us how to love. I usually have several such people in my life at any given time, and also realize I'm probably that person for someone else, so the message is always apropos.

Up to Christmas Eve the only "carol" Catholics sing is the dirgelike "O Come, O Come Emmanuel." Here at St. Basil's—and, I'm thrilled to contemplate, at Catholic churches around the world—Christ has finally been born, and a happy moment it is to finally break out in "Joy to the World" and "Angels We Have Heard on High." Glenn's been making asides the whole service, and Joan and I have been snuffling into our sleeves, and afterward we all congregate in the dark and cold on the side of the church, stamping our feet and looking a little sheepish in our Sunday-best sports coats and skirts and the hair we've actually combed for once, because after all it is Christmas Eve. The more thoughtful among us give Father Terry a paper-wrapped CD of Martinů or Bartók or Stravinsky. Then we walk over to BCD Tofu House for seafood hotpot and barley tea and commiserate because we're too misfitlike to have regular families.

It's not much, our motley little group. For a couple of years, we met at Judy's beautiful Craftsman house in Hancock Park, and sat in front of the fire, and drank peppermint hot chocolate out of porcelain cups. Then she (unfortunately) moved and we started converging on a back room in the rectory at St. Basil's, which is windowless and, but for the touched-up portraits of mostly deceased (and what appear to be at least 80 percent homosexual) priests, feels like a dentist's office. Someone's always late, someone's usually too loud, or goes on too long, or not long enough, or says something that doesn't make sense. Terry repeats himself, we repeat ourselves, sometimes we're uninspired or restless. We have cookies during Advent, and orange juice during Lent.

It's not much, and yet something happens in these little gatherings. This may be the closest thing to the early Church, to Christ and his disciples, we have, to go around the room, listening to each person share in turn, and hear, "I'm just getting out of a terrible months-long obsession with my masseuse. I have never undergone such pain in my life and, I know it sounds weird, but I'm really starting to get that . . . God is my lover." Or "My developmentally disabled son has gotten his developmentally disabled girlfriend pregnant. I'm afraid for the baby, but they're good people, and I have to remind myself—it's not the first time in the world a baby has been born to imperfect parents." Or "I saw some Ming vases at the County Museum the other day and they were so beautiful, tears came to my eyes. And I thought, *Oh my God, maybe there's hope. Maybe I'm not*

*a complete fake and a sham of a human being. Maybe I really
do have the capacity to love."*

To me, this sharing, this bearing witness, is the bread of life.
As it did when Christ turned water into wine, healed the leper,
miraculously multiplied the loaves and fishes so that all were fed;
for once, it feels as if there's enough. As happens when I partake
of the Eucharist, I feel the evidence of and corroboration of
another dimension, where whatever in me that has been lost is
found, where the parts of me I've corrupted and defiled are made
pure. I don't struggle with the urge to drink anymore, but I struggle every day with the urge to lapse into resentment, terror, a kind
of monstrous, free-floating restlessness that, if I don't tend to it,
will eventually lead to a drink. This is what will keep me sober:
this spark of light in others and myself, expressed in a way that
is neither corny nor sentimentalized nor melodramatized: this
reality that I wouldn't miss for anything in the world.

Still, I often think, really, I should be able to give a better
account of myself. With all the inner and outer work I've done—
the moral inventories and confessions; the trudging to jails,
hospitals, homeless shelters to talk to other drunks; the thousands
of hours of sitting with other alcoholics, of going to Mass, of wandering, reflecting, praying, writing, aching for what's wrong with
the world, for the suffering of the world, for my own suffering,
wishing I could relieve it—it seems I should have so much more
to show. It seems I should be so much more sane, healthy, balanced, selfless. But we followers of Christ do not get to look good,
sound good, make sense, convince people we are right: we get to
appear confused, bereft, clueless, frustrated, lonely. The truly
bereft and lonely will hear us, will find their way to us, to Christ

and his message and the people who try in their tiny way to love him. Our task is simply to be here, to keep ourselves in shape to welcome whoever does come. And to act in a way that's in accordance with what we say we believe, knowing we will always fall short. I have to remind myself that whatever else happens, I have done something with my life: I got sober. And as I'm staying sober—I mean sobriety in the larger sense, whether it's writing, washing the dishes, or hanging out with Father Terry and our crowd—I'm helping every other alcoholic/addict on earth who's struggling, whether sober and clean or not. In some small way, I'm helping every other human being to carry his or her cross.

So it's not much, our ragtag Lent and Advent group, and yet it's everything. Simply showing up, taking my turn during the readings, paying attention to Terry, listening quietly to what the other person has to say, and allowing myself to take pleasure in being acknowledged for my little say have so much value. To be with other imperfect people and, if only for an hour and a half, to catch a glimpse of their perfection—to rejoice with them, delight in them, know the other person is part of me, and I'm part of them, and that we all struggle, so hard and so long, with the same things, and still find the strength to keep going, keep searching, keep trying to be kind—this is the glory of our lives on earth. I get a glimpse of the paradise Dostoyevsky imagined in "The Dream of a Ridiculous Man": a place where "not only in their songs but in all their lives [people] seemed to do nothing but admire each other."

To say that Terry is an avid classical music fan would be something of an understatement. If he has a fault, it's that he can sometimes go on just a tad too long, and—I hesitate to say it—even get a little prideful, about his sound system, which, just for the record, includes a Prima Luna preamp, a Musical Fidelity power amp, and a pair of Quad 989 electrostatic speakers. Recently he had a bunch of us up to his apartment, put on Mitsuko Uchida playing Mozart's Sonata in A, and settled back, taking such obvious pleasure in the music he might almost have been playing it himself. Looking over to see him surveying us with the fond eyes of a shepherd guarding his flock brought tears to my eyes, and restored me, and made me know that life is worth living. It is worth living just because it has that Mozart sonata in it, and because there is a Mitsuko Uchida who played it, and a Msgr. Thomas Terrence Richey who loved it, and is passing it—and everything else he has lived for—on to the world, and for all the people who leave us with meat and drink for our souls. Most of all, of course, because of Jesus, from whom devoted priests and everything else flows.

Lost in thought, I felt an elbow in my ribs. "*Look* at him," Glenn stage-whispered from beside me, gesturing toward the good father. "Drunk again!"

CHAPTER 18

Never think that change is easy or that it comes suddenly or without pain. That is a storybook world. We are each the one to whom the question is addressed, "Do you want to recover?" ... It is a strange and frightening discovery to find that the sacrificial life that Christianity is talking about is the giving up of our chains—to discover that what binds us is also what gives us comfort and a measure of feeling safe.

—Elizabeth O'Connor, *Search for Silence*

One thing I can't figure out is how some people have no belief in or concern about God at all and appear to get along just fine; to make their way through life way more easily and suavely than, for instance, me. I'm always asking, How crazy would I be if I *wasn't* constantly consulting my spiritual director, and praying, and examining my conscience, and begging for God's mercy? You might be thinking—I've thought it myself—that all that stuff is *making* me crazy. But you'd be wrong. I'm not nearly as crazy as I used to be, when I had to drink basically every waking moment in order to function. I'm not nearly as crazy as I was when I had tens of thousands of dollars in the bank and was picking plastic bottles off the street to refill rather than spring 79 cents for a fresh Crystal Geyser. I could just be trying to make myself feel better, but it seems to me that the very purpose of my "spiritual path," for lack of a better term, is to bring us face-to-face with how wacked-out and unhinged we are, how desperately in need of help, how consistently we'll pursue the wrong plan, person, way of thinking.

I'm beginning to see that the whole of Christ's teachings can be read, or are perhaps most properly read, psychically: as a call to come awake. More and more, for example, I see I've walked around all these years almost completely unconscious of what drives me: of my deep agitation and unrest, of the perverse ways I sabotage myself. Driving around town like a maniac, never allowing myself enough time, knowing when I should leave but subconsciously finding something to do so I short myself ten minutes, so that for the whole trip I'm in a coma of adrenaline-charged anxiety and rage. Putting off my "happiness" until such and such happens: when I have a certain amount of money I'll be happy, when I sell a book I'll be happy, when I lose that last 2.38 pounds I'll be happy. The whole panoply of unexamined assumptions that are hardwired so deeply into my nervous system and psyche I don't even know they're there: I'm bad, I'm guilty, I'm unworthy of love.

Being awake, in other words, really means being awake to my motives, actions, thoughts: how they lead me astray, how they keep me stuck, how I often *like* them to keep me stuck. As a friend of mine recently said: "All my life I thought I was open-minded. 'I'm open-minded,' I'd tell myself. 'I live in a hip part of town, I have liberal politics, I'm a starving artist.' I had no idea how closed down I was, of the sense of grievance I walked around with, of how quick I was to think I knew who you were,

to judge." He was right: I focus on other people's defects so I don't
have to focus on mine. I resist admitting I'm loveable because
then I might have to love someone else. I stay attached to my
neuroses because I don't want the responsibility of being free.

Still, one thing that makes me think I might be on the right
path, or at least some path, is that I've started to notice how the
right book, person, situation are constantly presenting themselves. Maybe when you're open in a certain way, *everything*
seems like the right thing. But as an example, I think of my
friend Paul, a white, Republican, world-renowned money man-
ager, whom I sometimes have to stop in midsentence as he's
telling me about the Friday-night dinners with D.C. dignitaries,
the wine and cigars, the talk around the ten-foot-long mahogany
dinner table to remind him, "Paul? You do know my idea of a
good time is going down to Skid Row and hanging out with a
bunch of ex-drunks, right?" But this is just what I mean, because
people are complicated and full of delightful surprises, and Paul
is also a Catholic, and produces PBS documentaries in his
"spare" time, and knows or knew seemingly everyone, including
Pope John Paul II, Mother Teresa, Joseph Campbell, and the
Dalai Lama. He also has his own personal 6,000-volume library,
including several shelves of contemplative mysticism, and reads
everything, including eclectic literary journals like *The Sun*,
where a few years ago he saw a piece of mine, got in touch, hired
me to do some writing and editing, and has become a dear
friend whose opinion I respect and judgment I trust, and who
has been generous and kind to me beyond measure.

I recently stayed for a week with Paul and his wife at their
500-plus-acre horse farm in Virginia. Here I learned that, in

addition to his other attributes, Paul gets by on about three hours of sleep a night, always looks great, is knowledgeable about and absorbed by a variety of subjects, and, in the many hours I spent with him, never once appeared to be stressed or grouchy. Perhaps this is the place to say that though I like to paint myself as an asocial, wandering, mendicant freak, in fact I clean up quite nicely, and can hold my own in conversation with just about anybody, and know how to act helpful, interested, charming, and grateful. Still, no matter where I am or who I'm with, my basic feeling about myself and the world is pretty much a giant Diane Arbus photo.

All of which led me, near the end of my visit, to turn to Paul and ask, "Don't you ever get depressed?"

He thought for a while (just the fact that he had to *think* said it all). "Let's see," he said finally. "About twelve years ago, the market took a nosedive. . . . I think I might have been depressed for a few days then."

I regarded him for a moment, then inquired, in a tone that was perhaps slightly shriller than necessary: "You have *never been depressed about your personal life?*"

"Nope, never," he replied; then, catching sight of my incredulous stare, he asked, "Why, have you? You're not depressed anymore since you stopped drinking, are you?"

"I'm *always* depressed," I replied witheringly—trying to be funny, but as it's also somewhat true, segueing straight into self-defense. "I mean I try not to *indulge* it," I quickly continued, "it's not like I *enjoy* being depressed. Besides," I sniffed, "there's only so much you can do. Because *I* think our temperaments are *blueprinted* on us."

I've worked hard to overcome my bias against rich people, but times like this bring it out. Due to my own lifelong sense of teetering on the edge of sanity, for years I thought my moral imperative was to hang out only with people who were poor, or borderline mentally defective; I secretly prided myself on my ability to bond with other poor-in-spirit folks. Though I'd obviously reached the point where I was able in all good conscience, for example, to accept rich people's money, hospitality, and food, I still didn't believe there was anything to be learned, especially spiritually, from one of them. So—*Yeah,* I stewed on my bed that night, *I think our temperaments are* blueprinted *on us. That Paul is a supernice, smart, hardworking guy, and thank God he's taken me under his wing, but he's just never known* real *suffering.*

Then the next morning, I had an epiphany. I was walking along Pot House Road, gazing out across the low rolling green hills of Middleburg, when a passage from St. Paul rose to mind: "Your inmost being must be renewed, and you must put on the new man" (Ephesians 4:23–24). In the Divine Office, it's the epigraph to Psalm 51 that's read every Friday at morning prayer: "Your inmost being must be renewed, and you must put on the new man." I'd read the line probably hundreds of times, and I'd always more or less reflexively thought: *Okay, "the new man," that means I have to concentrate on being less selfish, more of service.* Kind of a kneejerk *No doubt about it, I definitely need to work on making myself kinder, more tolerant, more patient.*

But this particular morning, all of a sudden my body flushed hot, then cold, and I thought, *Maybe that's not what it means at all.* This morning I thought, *What if I'm not naturally depressed? What if I'm not naturally poor in spirit? What if my entire psyche*

were washed clean and I quit feeling guilty and ashamed; what
if I believed I really had been forgiven? What unimaginable
freedom might I enjoy if I ceased thinking of myself as con-
genitally damaged and defective? All my life I'd gone around
thinking, *Too bad for me, I was born under a black cloud! Too*
bad, we all have a cross to bear, and emotional fragility is mine!
But what if it were all an illusion? What if it were all just a
manifestation of my oh-so-inflated ego? What if I'd just been
protecting myself: from taking risks, yielding control, having
some fun? What if I could just pick up my mat, like the paralytic
Jesus cured—and walk?

In the following weeks I continued to mull this over. I love
that the people in the Gospels are so real, so much like me; and
I love that Jesus got right down and ate with them, looked at
and listened to them, touched their eyes and ears and healed
them—but only if they'd demonstrated that they were willing
to be healed. Like the woman at the well who was willing to
stop sleeping around and start drinking the "living water" that
would really quench her spiritual thirst (John 4:1–26). Or the
centurion who commanded his own army but humbly asked
Christ to heal his slave (Luke 7:1–9). Or the demoniac who threw
himself onto the fire and foamed at the mouth, about whom
Christ said, "This kind [of possession] can come out only through
prayer" (Mark 9:17–29).

How could I demonstrate my own willingness to be healed,
I began to wonder; how could I cooperate with Christ? What if,
for example, I could try to train my mind not to obsess? Or
discipline my thinking so as to avoid negativity? Staying awake,
choosing the light, takes effort: so much easier to lapse into a

coma of addiction, or depression, or sickness, or obsession, or despair! *The Cloud of Unknowing*; St. John of the Cross's *Ascent of Mt. Carmel*; Thomas Keating's *Open Mind, Open Heart:* these books on prayer and meditation are sacred texts. Too often my depression consists of an almost frantic lack of acceptance, a sullen resistance to what simply is. "Very truly, I tell you, before Abraham was, I am," Christ said (John 8:58). I am the ground of all existence; in other words, I am reality itself. What might be the effect on the world of a single heightened consciousness, a consciousness in utter accord with Christ?

On the other hand, I can't "put on the new man" by an effort of will. I don't have to try harder, I have to resist less. I have to be willing to be continually surprised, surprised anew each day; ever willing to try a new way and to let the old way go. I have to be willing to let go of all notion that a better, happier, more successful, more pain-free life exists in some other universe and that I'm missing out on it by virtue of bad luck, a malevolently withholding God, or even my own character defects. My sins themselves are a part of this universe, with all its darkness and all its light, all its pain and all its joy. When it comes to others, I have to be willing to let go of all notion of presuming to know how another person thinks, what he or she has suffered, is driven by, struggles with, has or has not overcome.

With all that, I have made *some* progress. Getting back to Paul, here is someone who, for much of my life, I would have been so closed down to and afraid of—either thinking I was better than or worse than him—that I would never have been able to fully respond when he appeared. I would have slunk about his beautiful house feeling like an intruder. I would have worried that he'd disapprove of my "politics" or that I'd disapprove of his. Instead, I got to attend a steeplechase, tour the National Sporting Library (a research center for horse and field sports, the only one of its kind in the world), be treated to several lovely dinners, and, under his watch, catch a glimpse of the next level of awakening. "From a certain point onward there is no longer any turning back," Kafka said. "That is the point that must be reached." I always imagined that meant the point where I would finally voluntarily offer myself at the stake, allow myself to be immolated, and officially become a martyr. But maybe it really means the point where I'll finally grow up.

Perhaps Paul's most wonderful attribute is that he is always giving me books, many by authors who are new to me. One such author is Helen M. Luke, an Oxford-educated Dante scholar who died in 1995 at the age of ninety. In a diary excerpt from her book *Such Stuff as Dreams Are Made On* she writes:

> An experience is not a mere outer happening or emotional reaction. It is something that an individual passes through consciously and learns from: "ex" means "out of" and "per" is also the root of "peril" and implies the presence of danger. An experience is born of a perilous happening which touches both conscious and unconscious and does not come to fruition without work and imagination. . . . [A]s soon as a burden of suffering is consciously accepted . . . then the years of unconscious suffering, neurotic suffering, become at once valid, and the consciously lifted burden is suddenly light and felt as a release. "*My* yoke is easy, *my* burden is light" [as Jesus said]. It is now carried by the Self, and the ego is released

from the crushing weight that is too great for it to bear. But the ego must be willing to carry it, to face the danger, to *experience* it, before this release comes.

The point of no return. Peril. Maybe the danger is that the deeper into myself I go in prayer, the more I try to discern God's will, the more I'll discover I'm nothing more than the broken-down alcoholic, drug-addicted, sex- and love-obsessed depressive I've always been. But sometimes I think about all the people in the world who really are in danger—of dying for their faith. Of starving. Of being blown up, or sexually abused, or killing themselves. So let me at least keep going—just in case something else turns up. Or in case I can somehow help already, by offering myself up exactly as I am.

CHAPTER 19

Truly Christian feelings are against human nature, they are abnormal, paradoxical. . . . We don't overcome our nature—it is replaced by some other, unfamiliar nature which teaches us how to be ill, suffer and die, and relieves us of the obligation to fear and hate.

—Abram Tertz, aka Andrei Sinyavksy, *Unguarded Thoughts*

One morning twenty years ago, I checked my face one last time in the bathroom I shared with the eight or ten other drunks who lived on my floor, stepped over a junkie nodding out in the hallway, and set out for my first day as a real-estate title examiner at Boston's Suffolk County Registry of Deeds. This might not have been much of a milestone for most people, but I was a newly sober thirty-four-year-old—with a law degree—who had never worked other than as a waitress. It was the first "real" job I'd ever had.

As I tightened my scarf against the February wind, the horror of my old life flashed before me: the nightly blackouts; the mornings scooping dead cockroaches out of glasses of stale beer; the bruises, from bad nutrition and constant falls, that covered my arms and legs. Law school had been a last-ditch attempt to achieve mainstream normalcy, but the whole three years I'd known that I was fooling myself; that there was no way on earth someone like me was ever going to go off every morning, with any degree of comfort, to a job that required wearing a suit and carrying a briefcase. Since the age of ten, my sole sense of direction had consisted in a private, stubborn urge to write. I'd taken a couple of classes at Harvard Extension, and kept a journal for years, but no matter how much I had thought about it, talked about it, planned to do it—without fail—the very next day, I had never been able to work up the nerve to sit down, face a blank page, and commit that first bold word to paper. Even six months of sobriety hadn't changed that. And in the meantime, I had to make money, had to start changing, had to start crossing the terrifying borders of a world I'd never been a part of.

Conscious that every step was bringing me closer to an unknown destiny, I crossed the cobblestones of Pemberton Square, climbed the wide granite steps of the old county courthouse, and pushed open the heavy glass door, its bronze handle burnished by a century and a half of sweaty palms. In the massive lobby, people streamed purposefully past in all directions, as if in a railway terminal. Amid those marble floors and three-ton cornices, I felt dwarfed, as inconsequential as an ant. After making several wrong turns, I found the elevator, a gilt cubicle with faded pink carpeting. In the corner stood a small, tough-looking man who looked as if he might have been a retired jockey.

"FLO-ah?" he barked as I stepped in.

"Beg pardon?" I said.

"FLO-ah!"

"Registry of Deeds," I stammered.

"FIFTH flo-ah," he singsonged. The car lurched precipitously down, shot up with a jolt, and, after an apparently motionless minute, came to a rest on floor two. This crawling ascent gave my anxiety plenty of time to ratchet itself up another few notches. I'd been over what to expect a hundred times with Marynia, the high-school friend from New Hampshire who'd helped me get the job. It sounded ideal: boss 20 miles away, laid-back Registry folks who left you alone—but I was so used to feeling guilty I was afraid I'd done something wrong before I'd even begun, and I couldn't help thinking of the way my last job had ended, when I'd had one too many shots of Wild Turkey before work, mouthed off to the cook, and he'd chased me out to the Massachusetts Avenue sidewalk brandishing a butcher knife.

"Reg'stry," the jockey announced, jerking the car to a halt, and I emerged into a room so long and wide and high it could have been a temple. The walls were lined with huge tomes bound in faded ocher leather, the marble ledges of the recessed windows were wide enough to sleep on, and, above rows of old-fashioned, inkwelled desks, a vault of space soared to a distant ceiling.

I spotted Marynia's blond head at a table near the back, and tentatively made my way in her direction. After years of working among people who came from "Dohchestah" and shopped at "Dan's Stah Mahket," Marynia had adopted her own exaggerated Boston accent as a kind of sick joke. She was always reporting that someone had "taken a haht attack" or "rearranged the pahlah," and, though she was a college-educated paralegal, childless, five years younger than me, and married to an architect, had taken to referring to herself as "Mothah."

"Welcome, dahlin'!" she said, patting the place beside her.

222 | *Heather King*

"Should we start working right away?" I asked shyly. "Or is it okay to eat first."

"Oh, *please*, hon, sit down! We'll have a nice chat." That was when I looked around and saw that people were scarfing down donuts, swilling cardboard cups of coffee, and, I was thrilled to note, sucking fiendishly away on cigarettes. At 7:30 A.M., the air was already blue with smoke.

I lit one myself, exhaled in relief, and held out the bag of muffins I'd picked up on the way. "Want one?" I asked Maryn.

"Not today, thank you," she replied modestly. "I'm reducin'." Then she leaned over, squeezed my shoulder, and whispered, "You stick with Mothah today. I'll show you just what to do."

Up to then, work to me had meant black rayon aprons reeking of onion rings and fried fish; blue cheese dressing beneath my nails; blistered, bleeding feet because going shopping for a new pair of shoes would have meant cutting into my drinking time. Just starting the day without a hangover was a revelation. I loved getting in early so I could read the *Boston Globe*, drink coffee, and enjoy a nice fresh Winston—sip, inhale, sip, inhale: heaven. The shelves of books, the harried recording clerks, with their time stamps and purple inked pads, the battered desks and chairs, evoked the timeless ambience of a library, one of the few places where I have always felt at home. Compared to my former life, working at the Registry was like being cast upon the shores of Shangri-la.

Over the course of the next few weeks, Maryn taught me not only the basics of title examining, but also such essential details as the location of the nearest Coffee Connection, which paper cutter made the cleanest edges, and the fact that you wanted to wait at least ten minutes after that elderly woman with the hennaed hair came out of the bathroom (this, too, was on a grand scale, the toilet on a raised dais, the sink as big as a bathtub) before going in yourself.

The purpose of the job was to clear titles for prospective real estate purchasers, and the mechanics consisted of marking the plot's dimensions on a numbered map and, with the aid of a series of grantor-grantee indexes, tracing the chain of ownership back fifty years. Sometimes, the plot had come out of a larger parcel and an even larger parcel before that, necessitating several different plans and a whole palette of colored pencils; or a chain of probates meant going back, occasionally over a hundred years, to a handwritten deed in wavering script that used stone fences or ponds or maple trees as boundary markers.

It didn't take long to get the hang of it. Within weeks, I, too, was joking around with "Fridge"—the hulking retarded youth who reshelved books—trading box scores with the guy who came in every morning with a suitcase full of rolls of quarters for the Xerox machine, and calling the office for my own assignments.

Once I learned the ropes, I completed my titles at breakneck speed, sprinting from one end of the cavernous room to the other, snatching indexes down from shelves, flipping through pages with the grim intensity of a Vegas blackjack dealer.

I did this partly to make the job more interesting, partly

because it helped me get in shape after years of sitting on bar-stools, and partly because I just like doing things fast. (Eventually I got so good I'd do all my work in the morning, stroll over to the Common after lunch, lie down, and take a nap on the grass.) But on another level, I ran because I was trying to make up for lost time, because I was trying to prove myself, because I was afraid if I stopped running it would all catch up with me again: the mornings drinking Sea Breezes with the old men at Sulli-van's Tap, the vodka nips for the subway ride to work, the reflection of my shell-shocked face staring back from the sides of industrial-size chowder pots and stainless steel coffee machines at the hash houses where I had worked. I had so little sense of myself I was afraid if I slowed down I might simply disappear. In that weighty new world of responsible jobs, and property ownership, I was a wraith, insubstantial as dust, a rootless plant ready to topple in the slightest wind.

Often a piece of land had come down through a will, or divorce decree, which meant a trip to the ground-floor probate department. Too impatient to wait for the snaillike elevator, instead I took the back stairs, slabs of foot-worn white marble which curved around flight after circular flight past mesh-covered windows and a view of the gritty courtyard. At the bottom, I'd stagger out to the hallway, queasy with motion sick-ness, race around getting the papers I needed, then head back up to the registry, my progress impeded by the sheer force of gravity. One morning, stopping to catch my breath somewhere around the third story, I paused and peered over the rail. The sight made me dizzy with vertigo—one misstep, one malevolent shove: a straight drop to a concrete floor. I thought of the thousands of nights I had wandered the streets alone, the mornings I had woken up in strange beds, the times I could have been raped or beaten or killed.

Alone in the echoing marble stairwell, I heard the sound of my breath, felt the quivering beat of my heart.

I was mortified not to be using my law degree, but my experience to date did not exactly make for the kind of resumé—or level of self-confidence—likely to attract the eye of a legal recruiter. And while I felt I should have been doing more "challenging" work, in fact there was an element to title searching I found almost addictively compelling. Its predictability and simplicity were precisely what I liked best: performing the same operations over and over again, with very slight variations, had a soothing effect on me, like a game of computer solitaire or a glass of gin. The irregular parcels of land with a jog here and there, the L-shaped ones we called "pork chops," the sprawling rural plots with streams and utility easements made for more interesting titles. But it was the symmetrical, bland, 50-by-90 housing development lots—four right angles, opposite sides equal and parallel—that flooded my weary heart with relief. The job exuded a sense of order and resolution my raw nerves craved: I hungered so strongly for order my hands trembled with it. The volume and page numbers, the marginal cross-references written in ballpoint, the grantor and grantee indexes, organized alphabetically and arranged by decade, anchored me safely to a world that had seemed, up to then, pure chaos. Nothing gave me quite the same sense of well-being as accounting for the interest of every devisee; finding that every mortgage, bankruptcy, and tax lien had been discharged; giving a piece of land a clean bill of health by writing on the final report, "Encumbrances: None."

Everything was new in those days: the smell of paper, sunlight streaming through fly-specked transoms, people. The Registry featured a colorful cast of characters. A woman with a voice like a carnival barker sold newspapers in the lobby, the bald-headed clerk with goiter came back from lunch every day trailing the fruity smell of bourbon, and Paul, the elevator operator, guided the doors open with an elegant flourish, as if piloting his passengers to the lobby of the Ritz. Joe, in charge of the plan room, was my favorite. He proudly displayed photos of his wife and children to complete strangers. He taught me how to do the perfect impersonation of a drunk—"Ya slur your words and stare at the *ear* of whoever you're talking to." Whenever the spirit moved him, he'd flick open his stapler, pretend it was a mike, and wander around his end of the room crooning Nat "King" Cole tunes: "Mona Lisa," "The Very Thought of You," "Stardust."

The Registry gave me the opportunity to be around people without having to interact with them at any taxingly deep level, and it was the perfect way to segue into the world outside of bars. The contact I had with my colleagues might have been superficial, but I had conducted my entire adult life without ever having learned to address a fellow human being minus the cushioning anaesthetic of four or five cocktails: for me, making small talk about the Red Sox and the weather under the influence of nothing stronger than caffeine was a major step forward.

I'd been semicomatose for so long it was like healing balm now to hear other people's voices, to study their faces, to watch the way their fingers gripped a pen. I felt like the man in F. Scott Fitzgerald's "The Lost Decade" who, coming out of a twelve-year binge, regards with wonder the cast in a waiter's eye, the backs of people's necks.

For all the titles I searched, I could never quite picture the houses on the land the ownership of which I tracked, could never quite conjure up the countertops and garbage disposals and walk-in closets of the mature, competent people who lived in them. Owning a home was a concept so far beyond my ken I literally could not imagine it: in spite of a grueling waitress schedule of double shifts and six-day weeks, what with pinball machines and jukeboxes, ludicrously huge tips for bartenders and cabdrivers, and my insatiable craving for alcohol, I had never put enough money together to even open a checking account. But who needed a house? To me, the $427 I took home every week was like winning the lottery: my rent was only $250 a month, I lived on Lean Cuisines and coffee, and the Boston Public Library had an endless supply of my beloved books. Discounting my student loan—which for the moment I had chosen to ignore—my salary was more money than I needed. For the first time in my life, I felt almost rich.

Thanks to Marynia, lunchtime was always an event. She'd organize the gals: Ruthie, the gentle one with epilepsy; Peg, who, at forty-six, still lived with her mother; me. Then she'd break out a vat of hummus or salsa, put together one of her "modulah" sandwiches—these had to be assembled just before eating so the bread wouldn't get soggy—and pass around a Tupperware container of brownies ("Helpy-selfy, homemade by Mothah!"). I'd eat my own slapdash meal of cheese and crackers to the soothing murmur of talk about baby showers and the price of bath mats, recipes for icebox cookies and American chop suey, the homely details of lives dedicated not to the furtive, frenzied scrabbling for the next drink, but to health, sanity, light. Maryn knew all about the sleazy bars, the one-night stands, the cockroach-ridden apartment, and accepted me anyway. But I found it astounding that I could slip so invisibly among the others: a regular person, not a pariah; a contributor, not a spreader of disaster and discord; a worker among workers, just like everybody else.

After the frenetic mornings, afternoons at the Registry were more leisurely, dreamier. The ceiling was twenty feet high, and through the tops of the windows I could see the sky: scudding clouds, a sun-shot sea of blue. Spread out below were the Customs House tower, with its pointy clock; the Government Square breakfast shop that had above its door a giant tea kettle that spurted gusts of real steam; the man who sold flowers—azure-crested birds-of-paradise, tulips the color of rubies—by the mouth of the State Street subway station. Beyond that were the Central Artery, pulsing with traffic through the city's heart; North Station with its pastry shops and spaghetti joints; the waterfront, smelling deliciously of salt, creosote, rotting fish.

I had lurched around those streets, blind drunk, for years, and I was finally learning how to see. I was storing all those details away, like a seed stores sunlight, allowing myself to feel the first faint stirrings of a desire that had almost, but not quite, died of neglect. It had been a long, long winter and, though I didn't know it yet, I was biding my time for spring.

It took me many more years, many more missteps, to find my bearings, but my time at the Registry was a foundation: the orderly titles walls of hope, Marynia's kindness a floor of faith, the days and weeks and months in which I learned to live— sober!—windows giving onto the view of a whole new world. Instead of looking to other people for validation, I could find it inside myself. Instead of holing myself up and off, I could take part. Instead of just working at some random job because I was too beaten down and narcotized to do what I longed for in the deepest part of my soul, I could count myself in and do work that I loved, work that made me feel alive and connected and whole, work that was not a prison sentence, but a kind of prayer.

I was in a blackout until I was thirty-four, paying off student loans until I was thirty-eight, forty-one before I wrote my first serious page. For a long time, I mourned the loss of those years. Now I wonder if I could ever have found my way without them. I wonder whether, as I meander around my apartment, my gaze would linger, as it still does now, on the rugs, the paintings, the mattress with sheets on it. I wonder whether I would have been so continually struck by the way that even our darkest, loneliest hours have buried within them the beginnings of grace. I wonder whether, if things hadn't unfolded exactly the way they did, I would have ever been given to discover that I was made to sit in a room for four or five hours a day thinking, dreaming, rearranging words. It is the only life I ever wanted, and it has given me a sense of abundance and possibility and being at home in the world beyond my wildest imaginings.

Marynia is a real mother now, with two daughters, twelve and fourteen. The last time I talked to her, she told me that the indexes have been computerized, that the shabby gilt elevator is automated now, that Fridge has moved on to a cafeteria job. In my mind, though, the Registry lingers on, as ageless as the light in a painting by Vermeer: the hunchbacked woman at the next table still using volume 6421 to jack up her seat, dust motes swimming in a vault of soaring space.

Toiling over an essay one recent afternoon in my Koreatown apartment, I thought of Joe, my old friend from the plan room. He was flicking open his stapler, waltzing through the Registry with his eyes closed, touching those things I used to touch—the crumbling leather spines of the grantor indexes, the pencil sharpener filled with cedar shavings, the unwieldy books of plans. I couldn't quite catch the melody he was singing—"A Blossom Fell," perhaps, or "Autumn Leaves"—but the listening distracted me just long enough so that, when I emerged from my reverie, the sentence I'd been working on stood fully constructed in my mind. As sound as a good roof. As impregnable as a notarized deed. As precious as a kingdom that's been paid for in blood—and that I own now: free and clear.

CHAPTER 20

Save all of yourself for the wedding though nobody knows when or if it will come.

—Carlos Drummond de Andrade

In my better moments, I can't believe I've made it this far. In my better moments, I remember eighteenth-century Jesuit priest Jean Pierre de Caussade writing, in *Abandonment to Divine Providence*, "I welcome every blow of his chisel as the best thing that could happen to me, although, if I'm to be truthful, I feel that every one of these blows is ruining me, destroying me, disfiguring me!" In my better moments, I remember a homily that Father Jarlath at St. Thomas the Apostle once gave about the time Jesus raised Lazarus from the dead: he said we all have things in us that are from the tomb—old rotting resentments, griefs, sorrows—and when it is time to look at them, it's a good idea to bring Jesus in with us. Nothing brings up those old griefs like aging. Taking stock. Realizing that we're never going to be done; we're going to die unfinished.

"Foxes have holes, and birds of the air have nests, but the Son of Man has nowhere to lay his head," Jesus said (Luke 9:58), and even if we've lived in the same place all our lives, that's true of all of us. We never really find a permanent resting place: we always have to be evolving, growing, changing; always have to be letting go, always have to be suffering various kinds of losses—which mount, the older we get. I know for every loss, there's a gain of some sort; a kind of richness, though I can't say I've experienced more than glimpses of it just yet. Maybe we grow into it, slowly. . . .

It's one of the greatest mysteries of all: time. What is it? Where does it come from? Where is it going? All my life I've seen time as the enemy; afraid there won't be enough time, racing against time, time running out, time that was aging me, diminishing my chances of happiness, success, love. But what if time were a friend, a tool, a gift? A gift in which for life to unfold, for things to ripen: friendships, situations, ideas?

When I started this book I thought I'd arrived somewhere, but now I realize I've barely, barely begun—as a human being, as a Catholic. I go to Mass on Sunday, and sometimes during the week. I pray the Psalms and readings of the Divine Office in the morning, and read that day's liturgy, and meditate on it for a while. I think of God, talk to him, ask for his help many times a day. At night, I usually try to reflect on the previous 24 hours, what I'm grateful for, where I could have done better. This last is often pretty horrifying, though the good news is it's often not as horrifying as it would have been ten years ago, or five, or even one. I go to confession in spurts; sometimes not for months, then three weeks in a row. I worry about the things we worry about here on earth: money, my work, whether I'll ever "find someone," my aging mother. I take my glow-in-the-dark rosary to bed with me, and every so often I wake with a start, tears of joy in my eyes, and I know . . . He's there.

What qualifies me to write a book like this—as a human being, as a Catholic? In a way, nothing. I could point to almost anyone I know and say they are more tolerant, more patient, more generous, calmer, braver than me. From the outside my life doesn't look much different than anyone else's, but on the inside it's permeated by Christ—physically, mentally, emotionally, spiritually. Inside, it's Christ who illumines it, blesses it, enriches it, gives it spiritual water and food and air. Outside, I sit in traffic jams and buy groceries at Trader Joe's; inside, my soul thirsts for him, my flesh "faints" for him, "as in a dry and weary land where there is no water," as the psalmist says (Psalm 63). To believe in the Transubstantiation is to make my way through the world knowing that someone sweat tears of blood for me in the Garden of Gethsemane the night before he died, was scourged for me, carried a heavy cross for me, was crowned with thorns for me, was crucified for me. That one day, in the cool of the garden, like Mary Magdalene, I will meet him, and cry, "Rabboni!" and fall into his arms, so that every moment on earth is a preparation to be worthy of that. This is what qualifies me: I love him.

At the same time, I keep in mind the parable where Jesus was talking to the crowds and someone came along and told him, "Look, your mother and your brothers are standing outside, wanting to speak to you." But to the one who had told him this, Jesus replied, "Who is my mother, and who are my brothers?" And pointing to his disciples, he said, "Here are my mother and my brothers! For whoever does the will of my Father in heaven is my brother and sister and mother" (Matthew 12:46–50). Tenderness is fine as far as it goes, in other words, but the proof of true tenderness is action: the willingness to change our lives, to lose our lives. "No one has greater love than this, to lay down one's life for one's friends" (John 15:13), and I have only to look at my own life, in which the effort required to, oh, say, answer a phone call can irritate me, to see how far away I am from that.

There is nothing winsome or goofy about God—or about the results for ourselves, and each other, of our failure to change our lives—and if there's a way of talking about God I find abhorrent, it's the way that says God is like a chocolate bar, God is a big teddy bear, God is the clouds in the sky. God is God of a world where drunks die in the gutter, and children get beaten to death by their mothers, and men are held indefinitely in cages, with hoods over their heads, and tortured: that's a place called Guantánamo Bay. I can't combat those things by pretending that they don't exist or that I don't have a part in them, or that God is "good" in the way we tend to think of good—"If God were good," as Meister Eckhart observed, "he could be better." I combat them by the long slow crucifixion of trying to love God with my whole heart, mind, soul, and strength, and my neighbor as myself: the hardest, most complex, paradoxical, maddening, stimulating, challenging, inexhaustibly enriching, perpetually unfinished, bound-to-fail, sublime task in the world.

I'm very struck by the line: "Those who love me will keep my word, and my Father will love them, and will come to them and make our home with them" (John 14:23). For long periods I'll feel like I'm just going through the motions, praying, saying the Psalms, trying to do the self-forgetful thing and knowing I'm doing a pretty bad job of it; doing my little kind of not very faithful, on-again, off-again fasting from whatever: gossiping, or swearing, or porn, and then one day maybe I'll look out the window in the morning and see the sun—the sun! that comes up every day, that has always come up, that will always come up—and I know . . . they have made their home in me. They have taken up residence in the deepest part of me.

It's October now, and the days are getting shorter, and I walk the streets looking at the sycamore leaves curling on the trees, the lilies of the Nile in the gathering purple dusk, and think, *Who am I that I should be so lucky, that I should have been allowed to be born, and to see the light on a fall afternoon in Los Angeles?*

Sometimes it seems as if what I long for is so far beyond what is here on earth, or that any person could give me, or respond to. And at the same time I see ever more clearly that I have never been really alone. I haven't missed anything and, in fact, all those untold hours, days and nights, years and years and years, when I have wandered around alone, yearning and aching, it was only for Jesus. "Nothing but Thee," as St. Thomas of Aquinas said . . . and now, because I have been alone so much in my life, what I had to build, and did build . . . I have something nobody can take away from me. It's been given to me, for better or worse, to spend a lot of time by myself in this vale of tears and I can't imagine what else I would do with it, or the universe wants me to do with it, or I could do with it, except to try to come more awake and alive, to learn how to love.

I was on retreat not long ago at a Cistercian convent in southern Arizona, walking through the desert; I hadn't talked to anyone in days. It was dead quiet, artemesia and mesquite stretching out on either side of the road, the sky Madonna blue. And I was suddenly struck with a thought that pierced my heart: I think I might have actually fallen to my knees. I thought, *Maybe God wanted to know us better*: maybe that's why he sent Jesus. Maybe he wanted to get closer to us: to understand more what it was like to be us, what we struggle with, how alone we feel, how conflicted we are, how deeply we long for peace, for connection. Maybe God himself longs for connection. . . .

Speaking of connection, I haven't said nearly as much as I could about my friends, partly because though I am always dying for someone to write about me, the people I've celebrated in print haven't been nearly as enthusiastic about my efforts. I will just say I wouldn't survive a day, whether they know it or not, without sharing in their struggles and triumphs; their plays, gigs, one-man-shows; their senses of humor. Take my friend Clam, who looks like a cross between Buddy Holly and Jack Benny, has a show called *Cut the Crap,* and conducts "self-help" seminars, the theme of which is "Helping you, help me, help you, is what it's all about!—I think?" Clam tells about the time his car broke down and he was laboriously trying to push it up an incline when suddenly the vehicle appeared to propel itself forward and effortlessly land on the crest of the hill. *It's a miracle!* Clam was thinking, when a small Mexican man—who, unbeknownst to Clam, had seen his plight and jumped in to lend a helping hand—sprang smilingly up from behind the hood; but as Clam says, it was a miracle either way.

A couple of years ago Clam gave me a book called *The Game of Life and How to Play It,* which was written in 1925 by, according to the jacket, "one of the most down-to-earth, practical, and helpful prosperity writers of her era": a woman named Florence Scovel Shinn. I scanned the table of contents, then noted, "Um, Clam? I think some people when they don't have money get a *job?*" To my surprise, however, Shinn's main model was Jesus— "Jesus Christ said, 'Seek ye first the Kingdom of God and his righteousness . . . You must act as if you *had already received"*— and the book was full of interesting stories. If you had only forty dollars left to your name, for example, the thing to do was not fearfully hoard it, but treat yourself and your friend to a fancy lunch, blow it in one fell swoop, and find a hundred-dollar bill lying on the sidewalk as you left the restaurant. If you were apartment hunting, the thing to do was not think, *Woe is me, nothing will ever turn up in this market,* but to buy some new blankets, secure in the faith that the apartment would soon materialize in which to use them.

But perhaps my favorite story was this: "Through misunderstanding, a woman had been separated from her husband, whom she loved deeply. . . . She made this statement: 'There is no separation in Divine Mind, therefore, I cannot be separated from the love and companionship which are mine by divine right.' She showed active faith by arranging a place for him at the table every day, thereby impressing the subconscious with a picture of his *return.* Over a year passed, but she never wavered, and *one day he walked in."*

I don't have a husband (at the moment!), but I'm almost always separated, to one degree or another, from my deepest self, and I'm reminded that it may be the hardest thing we have to do as humans. To be patient. To have faith. To not give up, to

238 | *Heather King*

not go through our days mad at everyone, or afraid of everyone, or wanting everyone to get out of our way, or in despair unto death because nobody's fixing us, nobody's giving us what we want, and our hearts are broken and shattered and bleeding, our hearts are stretched on the rack with longing, and we don't have the words to say it, and if we did, who would hear them, and we cannot bear *one more second* of it without picking up a drink, or a drug, or a gallon of ice cream, or shopping, or work, or fantasy, or a slot machine, or a gun.

So—Southern California wack job? Crossed the thin line between passion and pathology at last? You be the judge. But the upshot is I've arranged a place at my table, beneath the chandelier in the formal dining room, where I pass by and glance over at it a hundred times a day. A royal blue and gold Mexican pottery plate, an olive green linen napkin, a sterling silver knife and fork, a bamboo place mat—all blessed, prayed over, wept over, knelt before, kissed; making room for whoever and whatever might want to be welcomed. It could be anything. It could be an idea for a new book, or the opportunity to give away a big pile of money. It could be sickness or death. It could be Christ himself, the bridegroom, come in glory. I know not the day nor the hour when the Master might come, nor what he might ask, so I'll go about my daily tasks holding nothing back, but saving *all* of myself for the wedding.

And now—I'm waiting.